A ROADMAP FOR
THE JOB HUNT

R. D. BENNETT

A ROADMAP FOR THE JOB HUNT

A Practical Guide to Mastering Interviews, Resumes, and Landing the Job

Snowhill America LLC

CONTENTS

1

INTRODUCTION

A job hunt remains the same whether you're looking for career growth, a higher salary, a new location, or it's your first time. Creating a strong resume, networking, interviewing, and negotiating offers are all essential steps to securing a new job.

The current job market is incredibly competitive. As a result, candidates not only need the required job skills but also the ability to communicate their value at the interview. Prospective job applicants now must create personal websites or online profiles on job boards besides the traditional resume to showcase their abilities. Resumes (once simple, one-page documents focused on listing job titles, responsibilities, and dates of employment) now also emphasize accomplishments and quantifiable achievements. The widespread use of Applicant Tracking Systems (ATS) now means that candidates also need to have standardized resumes containing specific keywords for each application to ensure their resumes even get to human eyes.

How we connect with people through networking has changed as technological advances have changed. Previously, networking relied on in-person interactions at events, conferences, and social gatherings. Business cards, face-to-face meetings, and word-of-mouth recommendations were the primary methods for building professional relationships. But with the advent of the internet and social media platforms, networking has transformed into a more accessible and efficient process. Today, professionals can connect with peers, mentors, and potential employers from around the world with just a few clicks.

Networking and an interesting resume are both crucial components of a successful job search and can significantly enhance your chances of securing job interviews. Then, once the right people see your resume and flag it as interesting, you must survive the interview. An interview is where a company determines whether your skills and qualifications are a good match and whether your personal qualities match their company culture and can fit in with the team.

A bad hire for a company can be costly when you calculate the cost of hosting an interviewee (travel, salaries for interviewers, technology costs) and the indirect costs associated with time spent reviewing and scheduling interviews. In addition, there may be a loss of productivity while employees are engaged in the interview process. So, there is often internal pressure to hire the right candidate quickly.

For many people, anxiety about interview questions, public speaking, and judgments from strangers can make the experience nerve-wracking. Adding to this is the pressure you put on yourself to perform well, the fear of rejection, and the worry over unemployment. It's no wonder that stress levels rise during a job search. Interviewing is like an audition, and if even seasoned actors admit to pre-performance nerves, it's no surprise that many of us feel anxious when interviewing is an occasional and high-pressure event. However, it's important to remember that an interview is a 2-way conversation. It's not just the company that gets to choose its next employee; you also get to choose your next employer. An interview is an opportunity for you to determine if the position is one that you want and that the company is one that you feel comfortable joining. On average, a person who works a 40-hour week for 48 weeks per year (assuming 4 weeks' vacation each year) for 43 years (ages 22 to 65) will spend 82,560 hours at work, not including overtime. As work can take up such a large proportion of your life, it must work for you too.

This book aims to simplify your job hunt. Every chapter provides practical steps to make your journey successful and provides the support you need to navigate your job hunt. Whether you're looking for a step-by-step guide or quick tips to refine your strategy, this book can help. From crafting a standout resume, sailing through interviews, or negotiating your salary, you'll find tools, tips, and strategies to help you every step of the way. By taking a focused and organized approach, you can confidently navigate the job hunt and land a role that aligns with your career aspirations and suits you.

You don't have to read this book cover to cover, so jump to the sections that are most relevant to where you are in your job search. If you're just starting, begin by crafting your resume and personal brand. Preparing for interviews? Dive into the interview preparation chapters. Wherever you are on your journey, you'll find tools to guide and support you.

On a personal note, I wrote this book after losing a job I had held for over 15 years. When I began interviewing again, I quickly realized how unprepared I was and felt overwhelmed by the endless advice on how to craft the perfect resume, navigating job applications, and excelling in interviews.

What started as simple notes to help me understand job search terminology and 'career coach' language gradually expanded. As I learned more about modern job search expectations, I added details and new sections. Over time, those notes grew into this book, an all-in-one guide that encompasses everything that I've learned, which I now wish to share with you.

So, I wish you all the very best on your job hunt journey. May you find opportunities that align with your passions, highlight your strengths, and lead you to success and fulfillment as quickly as possible!

2

THE JOB SEARCH

Conducting a successful job search requires strategy, persistence, and organization. To help narrow down the job opportunities, define what kind of work environment and company you're looking for. Also, identify your strengths and weaknesses to help determine the role that best suits you. This will help you understand what you can offer a company and highlight any areas that you need to improve while you look for a new job.

The internet has made life easier for job seekers as popular online platforms have made job searches more effective. Platforms that post a wide range of job types include Indeed, LinkedIn, Glassdoor, and ZipRecruiter. While there are platforms for more specialized roles, such as tech (Dice, AngelList [startups] or Stack Overflow), creative (Behance, Dribble, or Mediabistro), nonprofit (Idealist or Devex), or remote jobs (We Work Remotely, Remote.co® and FlexJobs). You can also find government jobs on USAJobs (for US federal positions) or regional government websites for local opportunities. Job openings and career advice may also appear on forums, social media groups, or platforms like Reddit and Slack communities specific to your industry. Many of these sites also allow you to receive updates on new postings that match your criteria.

Many companies also post their job openings on their corporate website. If there's a specific company you like to work for, you may be able to set up alerts for any new job postings.

The start of your job search is the best time to prepare for interactions with recruiters and companies. Identify a telephone number and email address for all job correspondence. Check your outgoing voicemail message to ensure it is professional as well as confirm there is space for new messages in your inbox. Also, consider which email address you will use; does it portray you professionally?

Remember, job searching is a process, and it might take some time to find the right fit. Stay focused, be proactive, and seek support from friends, family, or career counselors.

FINDING THE RIGHT JOB

Before getting to the interview stage, you must identify the type of position you are looking for. Finding the right job is a blend of self-reflection, research, and strategic planning. Consider your skills and interests so that you can match your strengths and passions with roles that align with your expertise. Do you want a specific type of role (remote, hybrid, on-site, etc.), or are there other factors that are more of a priority (salary, growth opportunities, location, company culture, etc.)? Look into industries that match your interests and skills. Use resources like LinkedIn, Glassdoor, or industry-specific sites to learn about various roles. Research industry trends to identify which fields have strong growth and demand patterns. Ask yourself where you want to be in 5–10 years. Do you prioritize your salary, growth opportunities, work-life balance, or the ability to make an impact?

To help keep you focused, creating a career plan can help you define your goals and provide a roadmap can help. It can also help you take advantage of any opportunities for growth and development when they arise. Once you have identified your goals, you can determine the difference between the skills you currently have, and the skills required for a desired job or career goal by performing a skills gap analysis. This will help you pinpoint areas for improvement, prioritize learning, and understand what's needed to qualify for a promotion or a new role.

After you understand the requirements of a new role, you can create a detailed career plan. A skills gap analysis is a powerful step towards defining your career development. Such an analysis can help you focus on meaningful progress toward your professional aspirations and potentially avoid unnecessary training.

Once you have identified your target role, you can then start to collect information to identify any common requirements for the role. You can also speak with people in the field to understand any expected qualifications. Compare your skills to the requirements of your target role by ranking your existing skills and certifications without overestimating or underestimating them (e.g., beginner, intermediate, advanced) using a skills tracker.

Example Of A Skills Tracker

Skill	Current Level		
	B	I	A
B= Beginner; I = Intermediate; A = Advanced.			

Then, highlight any missing skills or areas where your proficiency is below what's expected. This will then allow you to focus on the skills that are most in demand for your target role and help you select relevant courses, certifications, workshops, or self-study materials. You can also gain hands-on experience through volunteer work, internships, freelance projects, or personal initiatives.

Knowing what skills you need and how to gain them will help you progress faster toward your goals. By bridging your skill gaps, you will be a step closer to employer expectations, thus making you a stronger candidate. Also, staying current on your skills ensures you remain competitive as job markets and industries evolve. Focus on the skills that are most in demand for your target role by selecting relevant courses, certifications, workshops, or self-study materials. You may also gain hands-on experience through volunteer work, internships, freelance projects, or personal initiatives.

Having a career plan in place helps you to prepare for any changes by helping you pinpoint the skills and qualifications required to achieve your goals. You should view a career plan as a living document, open to change to accommodate unexpected career shifts. If you need help to craft your career plan, working with a dedicated career coach may be beneficial.

Finding a job that matches all your requirements in a tough employment market can be difficult, so you may need to prioritize your wish list and be open-minded to the available opportunities. But knowing your long-term goals can make it easier to stay motivated even when faced with challenges. Remember, every job has the potential to contribute to your career growth, no matter how small.

Finding positions that match either your short or long-term requirements will ensure your interest and enthusiasm for the position will shine through in the interview.

Example of a Career Plan

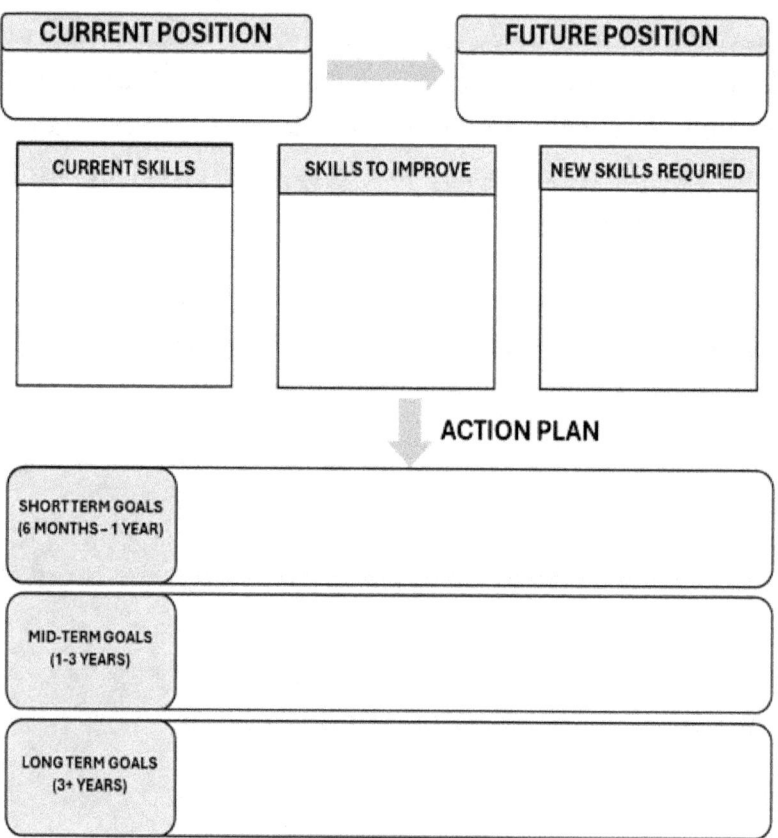

Example:

Career Goal: Become a marketing manager.

Required Skills: Team leadership; marketing analytics; budget management; SEO and content strategy.

Current Skills: Marketing analytics (intermediate); SEO and content strategy (advanced); social media management (advanced).

Gaps Identified: Team leadership; budget management.

Action Plan: Enroll in a leadership course and seek mentorship opportunities. Take a workshop on financial planning for marketers within the next 3 months.

WHAT TYPE OF JOB

There are a variety of work arrangements that can work for different lifestyles, goals, and industries. When deciding which suits you, consider your lifestyle needs, financial and career goals, and your preference for the work environment. Assess the advantages and drawbacks of each option before choosing a specific type of role. It is also important to evaluate the complete employment package, as companies may offer employees access to health insurance, retirement plans, paid time off, and opportunities for promotions and professional development, which may impact your decision.

Full-time Work

Full-time status is a fixed schedule standard arrangement that involves 35 to 40+ hours per week. The benefits of full-time work are consistent income and long-term employment. The lack of flexibility in the work schedule can make achieving a work-life balance more demanding, depending on the role and industry.

Hybrid Work

Hybrid work allows employees to split their time between the workplace and home. This can allow for a greater work-life balance while maintaining in-person collaboration. The challenges are that you may need to provide an internet connection yourself and align your schedule with other team members.

Work from Home (Remote Work)

Work-from-home status is the ability to work remotely from an office location full-time. The benefits can include no commute time, more control over your work environment, and the potential opportunity to work for companies located anywhere. The challenge is that corporate office requirements may dictate your schedule, thus limiting your flexibility. Because of the lack of face-to-face interaction, you may also feel more isolated from not having the same level of social interaction as you would be in the office. Some companies require separate childcare to be available to ensure focus, as home environments can introduce challenges to focus and productivity.

Part-time Work

Part-time work involves working for fewer hours per week (e.g., under 35 hours). Part-time work may be easier to balance with other commitments, like education or caregiving, because of the reduced hours. This option may also be useful for gaining experience or transitioning into a new industry. The challenge, however, is that these positions often lack health insurance or retirement contributions, and your earnings may be lower and less predictable.

Contract Work

Contract work is typically for a specific period or project that is organized through a staffing agency or directly with a company. One benefit of contract work is that you can choose contracts that align with your career goals, helping you build your experience in a specific

field or project. Occasionally, some contracts may even lead to permanent roles. Another benefit may be the option to take extended breaks in between contracts, although this depends on the length of each contract. The challenge is that your contract's completion ends your employment, limiting your income to the contract's duration. In addition, contracts often exclude health insurance or paid leave.

Consulting

Consultants provide expert advice or services to organizations on a temporary or project basis. Because consultants work with diverse companies, industries, and challenges, they can gain extensive experience allowing them to command premium rates for their expertise. Consultants also often have the freedom to choose their clients and projects. The challenge is that the work depends on demand and reputation, thus the income can be unpredictable. In addition, some consulting roles may require frequent travel to client sites.

Freelancing

Freelancers are self-employed individuals who offer specialized services to clients on a project or hourly basis. The benefits of freelancing include having control over your clients, projects, and schedule. You also can work on diverse projects with multiple clients, while higher earnings may be possible depending on your skills and reputation. The challenge is that the income may be inconsistent, as work may be sporadic with periods of low demand. Also, freelancers must handle taxes, invoicing, and marketing themselves.

YOUR ONLINE PRESENCE

A strong online presence may be the one thing that helps make you stand out from other candidates in a competitive job market. It can show why you're the ideal fit for a role or company. This can be especially important for creative fields like design, writing, and marketing, where being online allows you to showcase your skills, experiences, and achievements. Here you can use a portfolio, blog, or social media posts to help you stand out from other candidates.

Maintaining a strong online presence can increase your chances of being seen by potential employers and recruiters. This allows employers to find you more easily, thereby expanding your reach and networking ability. Having an online presence also allows you to follow industry leaders, business influencers, and companies online. This can help you stay informed about trends, news, and developments in your field, so making you a more knowledgeable candidate. By sharing professional and positive content related to your industry, such as articles, blog posts, taking part in discussions, and sharing your insights, you can hopefully attract the attention of recruiters and hiring managers.

Online platforms previously used only for personal connections are also now being used professionally. For example, on Facebook, you can interact with companies via their homepage newsfeeds, or "Like" posts. Individual industry leaders may also have their own personal blogs to which you can subscribe. Facebook messaging can also be used to build relationships like LinkedIn. Many companies are also on Instagram, which allows you to review the company's culture as well as interact with them.

Job postings are now being made on X (formerly Twitter) by both companies and recruiters, with the job sections having their separate usernames.

Ensure that you present a consistent tone of voice and messaging when using multiple online platforms. The information you present, including any visual elements, should be the same across all platforms. This includes your resume details, job titles, dates of employment, and other professional details. Be in control of your online posts, and if possible, tag photos to maintain your image. Also, use keywords that support Search Engine Optimization to support your brand.

Cleaning Up Your Online Presence

Many companies will use the internet as a fast and inexpensive background check. Companies can search your social media sites to verify your resume and check out your knowledge and publicly expressed attitudes. It is therefore advisable to search for your own name before you start your job hunt to see what potential employers might find and to make your profile private unless it is suitable for professional use.

Be sure to review your Social Media profiles (Facebook, X, Instagram, LinkedIn, etc.) for any "digital dirt". Remove any posts, photos, or comments that might be unprofessional or controversial, and adjust your privacy settings to control what others can see. Update all your profiles to ensure they contain the most accurate information. Also, use a consistent and professional profile picture across all platforms. Examine photos and posts where you're tagged and remove tags from anything you dislike. If you have old social media accounts or profiles that you no longer use, consider removing them or deactivating them.

For unprofessional posts that you cannot hide or delete, you can try to "bury" them by increasing the number of professional posts and moving the more negative posts down on your timeline. Consider setting up Google Alerts for your name to monitor any new mentions of you online to address any potential issues quickly. If needed, you can differentiate yourself from others by slightly changing your profile name (e.g., adding your middle initial.)

If needed, online companies such as Scrubber, BetterReputation, and NetReputation can help clean up your social media profile and assist individuals in maintaining a professional and positive online image.

By following these steps, you can ensure that your online presence is professional and reflects positively on you during your job search.

LinkedIn

For business, LinkedIn is currently one of the most popular global professional networking and career development platforms available. It is free to use (a premium option is available for a fee) and can be a powerful tool in your career path. It allows you to research companies and people and search for jobs on one site. To help showcase your professional background, you can also create a personal profile where you can post the same information as what is on your resume (i.e., job history, education, professional training, certifications, and skills) and highlight any key achievements.

When using LinkedIn, it is important to ensure your profile is up-to-date, professional, and optimized with relevant keywords in your headline to highlight your potential fit for positions. While job-seeking, the key sections of your profile to complete are your Headline, About, and Experience sections. Your LinkedIn profile must align with your resume, as many employers will review your LinkedIn profile as part of the screening process.

An important component of your LinkedIn profile is your photo in the Headline Section. Your headshot is often the first impression you make on potential employers, clients, or network connections and forms an important component of your branding. Profiles with photos receive significantly more views and connection requests than those without, so your photo should be a recent, high-quality, professional photo to help convey that you take your career seriously.

Highlight your current role or key expertise in the Headline section. The About Section should list your career journey, achievements, and goals concisely and engagingly. The Experience and Skills sections should include measurable results and relevant keywords. It is also helpful to request endorsements from colleagues to boost your credibility; these will appear in the Recommendations section.

Following 4 to 5 groups related to your industry or interests can help keep you connected with the latest trends, news, and developments in your chosen field. If there is a specific company you are interested in, you can follow it and interact with its content to show interest.

LinkedIn allows you to connect with professionals in your industry, former colleagues, alumni, and potential employers. These connections can lead to new opportunities and collaborations by increasing your visibility. Sharing your expertise, achievements, and insights by posting content and engaging with others can help establish you as a thought leader in your industry. Having and making recommendations and endorsements on the platform can also help establish and build your credibility. LinkedIn offers educational resources, including articles, webinars, and courses that may help you develop new skills and advance your career, although some of these are only available through the premium option.

Whether online, in-person, or during interviews, a polished personal brand is essential for making a powerful impression. By consistently presenting yourself as a professional who aligns with the roles you seek, you increase your chances of standing out and securing your next opportunity.

MINDSET AND MOTIVATION

A successful job hunt requires more than resumes and interviews. It also hinges on a positive mindset and sustained motivation. The process can be stressful, especially when faced with rejection or long waiting periods. Staying mentally strong and focused is essential for navigating your job hunt.

Once you understand anxiety is a natural part of the job hunt, don't let it control you. Stay calm and direct your energy toward actions like improving your resume, applying for jobs, and preparing for interviews rather than worrying about outcomes.

View rejection not as a personal failure but as a learning experience that brings you closer to the right opportunity. By acknowledging the little steps like completing applications, landing interviews, or making new connections, you reinforce the progress you are making. Be sure to lean on friends, family, or professional groups for encouragement and advice, as sharing your journey, the good and the bad, can help to reduce stress and build your confidence.

To help manage your job search, break it down into achievable tasks using the SMART framework (Specific, Measurable, Achievable, Relevant, Time-bound). For example, create tasks like applying for five jobs per week or attending one networking event monthly.

Treat your job hunt like a job by setting a daily schedule to work on it. Address applications, skill-building, and follow-ups during this time and leave time to relax to avoid burning out. Picture yourself succeeding in your next role, as this will help boost your confidence and keep you focused on the end goal. Remember to take breaks to recharge both mentally and physically. Anxiety over slow progress can lead to frustration and reduced effectiveness, so it is important to maintain a sense of normalcy to avoid the search becoming all-encompassing by celebrating your progress, no matter how small, and taking time to relax.

A positive, resilient approach not only improves your well-being but also helps you present your best self to potential employers.

3

BUILDING A RESUME

A resume provides a concise and organized summary of your qualifications, experiences, and skills to potential employers. It is the preferred format for corporate jobs in the US, Canada, and Australia. People primarily use it for private-sector jobs (such as business, technology, and creative jobs). Often, your resume is the first introduction you make to a prospective employer to show your suitability for a specific job by providing a quick snapshot of your capabilities and encouraging hiring managers to invite you for an interview. Interviewers will often use it as a source of reference during the interview.

A resume summarizes only the most relevant details for a specific job application and is typically 1 to 2 pages long. A well-laid-out resume should highlight your education, work experience, skills, and achievements relevant to the role. It should create a strong first impression by emphasizing your most relevant accomplishments in an easy-to-read format. Often, written in a reverse chronological or functional format, a resume focuses more on your recent experience. It is beneficial to tailor your resume to each position that you apply for so that you can highlight your relevant experience and skills to the job description and company needs and include relevant keywords and formats to increase the chances that your resume passes any Applicant Tracking Systems a company may be utilizing.

A well-crafted resume reflects your attention to detail, communication skills, and professionalism.

CV OR RESUME

Although people often use the terms CV (Curriculum Vitae) and resume interchangeably, especially in Europe, Asia, and Africa, these two document types serve different purposes.

A CV is a comprehensive document that is used primarily for academic, government, research, medical, and international job applications. It focuses on the complete history of an individual's professional and educational background.

A CV is typically 2 to 5 pages long, but depending on a person's experience and achievements, it can be longer. It includes details of work experience, publications, presentations, credentials, and long-term accomplishments. A CV organizes your entire career chronologically. When you need to highlight your complete academic and professional background, a CV is the best option.

CV and Resume Contents

Element	CV	Resume
Focus	Comprehensive career history	Relevant skills and experiences
Work Experience	Detailed, including all roles	Selective, highlighting relevant roles
Education	Extensive, listing all qualifications	Summarized, focusing on key degrees
Skills	Broad overview of all competencies	Targeted to the job role
Achievements	Detailed list (publications, awards, research)	Brief, results-orientated statements

APPLICANT TRACKING SYSTEMS (ATS)

Applicant Tracking System (ATS) is a software application used by companies to streamline the hiring process. It acts as a digital gatekeeper, managing job applications, sorting resumes, and helping employers find the best candidates. Understanding how ATS works is crucial for jobseekers because a significant percentage of companies, especially larger organizations, rely on these systems to manage high volumes of applications. ATS allows companies to focus on the most qualified candidates, making the process faster and more organized.

How Does ATS Work?

Employers use ATS to create, post, and manage job listings on company career pages and third-party websites. It enables recruiters to send automated emails, schedule interviews, and track candidates throughout the hiring process.

ATS stores resumes and cover letters in a centralized database. It organizes applications by parsing key information, such as contact details, work history, education, and skills. The ATS scores and ranks the resume based on their alignment with job requirements. As a result, hiring managers may often review only the top-ranking applications.

Optimizing Your Resume For ATS

To increase your resume's chances of a high score, tailor it to each job by including specific keywords from the job description. Avoid using images, graphics, or complex layouts that ATS may not process correctly. Use standard section headers like "Work Experience" and "Education" and include a dedicated "Skills" section with both hard and soft skills relevant to the job. The preference is for simple, professional fonts like Arial, Times New Roman, or Calibri, with electronic copies of your resume submitted as PDF or Word documents (doc or .docx) or in a format required by the company.

By optimizing your resume for ATS, you ensure it gets seen by the people who make hiring decisions.

KEYWORDS

Search Engine Optimization (SEO) for keywords in the job hunt context refers to the strategic use of relevant keywords in your online profile. These keywords, when used in your resume, cover letter, LinkedIn profile, and online applications, can increase your visibility to recruiters, hiring managers, and Applicant Tracking Systems (ATS). Just as SEO helps websites rank on Google, using the right keywords can help you stand out to potential employers. As many companies use ATS to screen applications, resumes lacking relevant keywords may not make it to a recruiter's desk. Therefore, highlighting the right keywords ensures recruiters see how your skills align with the role, as well as demonstrating that you have read the job description and customized your application.

LinkedIn also uses keywords to match profiles with job postings similar to how Google search functions. As many recruiters search for potential candidates online, including relevant keywords in your resume can help recruiters find your profile when searching for candidates with specific skills or experience. Using the same keywords on your resume, LinkedIn profile, personal website, and your portfolio should make you easier to find.

Using Keywords Effectively

Review several job postings in your desired field and identify the keywords most used to identify the optimal keywords. Google Trends or other keyword research tools can help you identify trending industry terms and phrases. Online tools like Jobscan can also analyze your resume against a job description and identify missing keywords.

Focus on hard skills, soft skills, qualifications, and job-specific terminology, and use the language and terminology specific to your industry or field.

Examples of marketing keywords might be "content creation," "SEO," "Google Analytics," or "social media marketing." For tech industry roles, keywords such as "Agile," "cloud computing," and "software development lifecycle" may be more relevant.

Incorporate the keywords in your resume or cover letter within the context of your skills, experiences, and accomplishments. By using specific examples, you can highlight experiences that align with the keywords you've identified. This will show how you've successfully applied those skills, improving your chances with both ATS and human reviewers. You can also use tags as keywords, which might better suit creative portfolios.

To optimize your LinkedIn profile, update your Headline and Summary sections to include industry-specific keywords. By doing so, this will improve your profile's visibility in search results. You can also add relevant skills to your LinkedIn profile that match the job roles you're targeting.

It is best to use action-oriented keywords and quantifiable results wherever possible. Action-oriented keywords such as "managed," "led," "developed," "designed," and "improved" can describe your accomplishments, while quantifying the impact of your work will add more substance and credibility to your statements.

Keywords should reflect both your technical and interpersonal skills. For technical skills, you can include specific technical abilities or tools relevant to the role (e.g., "JavaScript," "financial analysis," "Adobe Photoshop"). While interpersonal "soft" skill keywords include "leadership," "communication," "problem-solving," or "team collaboration".

To keep the keywords relevant, only use those that apply to the job you are applying for. Misleading or irrelevant keywords can hurt your credibility. It is also best to check that the keywords are still current, as job market trends and keywords can shift. Therefore, update your resume, LinkedIn, and other professional profiles to stay aligned with current demands. Be sure to review your resume, as overloading your application with keywords can feel unnatural and affect the flow of your resume or cover letter.

By using SEO principles for job search keywords, you can optimize your application materials to align with what employers are looking for, increasing your chances of landing your dream role.

CORE COMPETENCIES

Core competencies are the specific skills, knowledge, and attributes that define your expertise. They are what make you qualified for a role. Highlighting them in your resume, cover letter, and LinkedIn profile is crucial for demonstrating your value to potential employers. As employers often view past performance as an indicator of future behavior.

Your core competencies are your key strengths. They can include technical skills such as job-specific abilities (e.g., programming, financial analysis, data visualization). As well as soft skills, such as interpersonal and transferable skills (e.g., communication, leadership, adaptability).

In addition, you can also include your expertise in specific fields or industries (e.g., marketing, healthcare, project management), or personal traits that enhance workplace performance (e.g., creativity, problem-solving, attention to detail).

Highlighting your core competencies can show potential employers how your skills align with the role. This helps them to focus on your most valuable strengths. By focusing on your strengths, you can differentiate yourself from other candidates. Keywords related to core competencies may also help improve your chances of passing the ATS screening of your resume.

Your resume is a good place to start when listing your core competencies. To highlight them, place them in a separate section and focus on your top 5–10 core competencies that are most relevant to the role. Incorporate strong action verbs (e.g., "led," "implemented," "analyzed") to describe how you've applied your skills.

Include the core competencies noted in the job descriptions in the Professional Experience section of your resume. This will help show how you applied them and the results you achieved. Including metrics also strengthens their appeal.

Example: *"Used advanced data analysis techniques to identify market trends, leading to a 20% increase in sales."*

In your cover letter, you can use specific examples to show how your core competencies meet the needs of the role.

Example: *"In my previous role, I leveraged my project management skills to lead a cross-functional team, completing a $1M project early and under budget."*

In your LinkedIn profile, you can also add relevant core competencies in the Skills section. Highlight key competencies with examples of how they've contributed to your career achievements in the About section. Also incorporate them into your job descriptions to add context and depth in the Experience section. As the relevance of your core competencies may change depending on the type of roles you're targeting, be sure to review them to confirm they are still relevant.

During interviews, be prepared to provide examples of how your core competencies have contributed to your success. Use the STAR method (Situation, Task, Action, Result) to do this.

Example: *"One of my core strengths is problem-solving. At my previous job, I identified inefficiencies in our supply chain (Situation), implemented a real-time tracking system (Task), and reduced delivery delays by 25% (Result)."*

You position yourself as a strong, qualified candidate who aligns with the employer's needs by showcasing your core competencies. Tailoring these strengths to each role ensures you stand out and communicate your value with clarity and confidence.

Examples of Core Competencies by Field

Field	Core Competence
Marketing	Content Strategy SEO Optimization Brand Management Market Research
Finance	Financial Modeling Budgeting and Forecasting Risk Analysis Regulatory Compliance
Tech	Programming (Python, Java) Cloud Computing Cybersecurity Data Analytics
Human Resources	Talent Acquisition Employee Relations Diversity and Inclusion Performance Management
Sales	Lead Generation Negotiation CRM Tools Sales Strategy

4

NETWORKING

Networking in business is the act of developing a positive relationship with individuals and businesses for a professional purpose. Networking can include making business-related referrals, contacts, and recommendations. Referrals often fill positions instead of job postings. Networking can also uncover many job opportunities. However, it requires patience as your initial network is unlikely to know of a job suitable for you immediately, but they may know someone who can help you, or they will remember your interaction in a few weeks when they hear of an opportunity. Networking is all about building long-term connections and the quality of your network rather than the quantity.

The art of networking is to build trust by showing sincere interest in others' work and experiences by being genuine and actively listening so that you can focus on what the other person is saying and ask meaningful follow-up questions.

For successful networking, it is best to start small and then build up your network as you gain confidence. Common challenges with networking are feeling awkward or shy, not knowing what to say, or the fear of rejection. To address these challenges, it is best to practice your introduction and prepare a few icebreakers, besides creating an elevator pitch. Focus on listening rather than talking and learn to reframe rejection as part of the process.

FACE-TO-FACE NETWORKING

Initially, networking may seem like an impossible task. But you can start by tapping into your existing network by letting your family, friends, and acquaintances know you are job hunting and asking for their advice. Reconnect with past coworkers, managers, and mentors as well. Volunteering or freelancing also offers opportunities to build connections and show your abilities to potential employers.

People are more likely to talk to you if there is no pressure, so focus on asking for advice, rather than them finding you a job. Also, offer help, share insights, or connect with others when appropriate. Networking is a two-way street. Go to a networking meeting with the view of learning more about the person you are meeting. Be positive in your outlook as well, as this will keep the conversation moving.

Even if you don't enjoy small talk, you can still network by focusing on the other person. You should plan for face-to-face networking meetings to last about 30 minutes. If they last longer, great, but if not, that's fine too. It's all about the connection.

Choose a quiet location so you can hear the conversation. Dress professionally and focus your attention on the other person. To limit distractions, put your phone away.

Before the meeting, prepare an introductory statement for yourself that describes your career goals, and the plan for the meeting (to ask for advice). Have a copy of your resume with you, but don't provide it unless asked. Face-to-face networking meetings are more about making connections and building relationships rather than formal job applications. If preferred, you can always include the resume with your follow-up email.

Depending on your relationship, break the ice for the first few minutes, but focus the meeting on building the relationship.

Before meeting with someone, make a list of 5 open-ended questions to ask to help get the conversation started. Suggestions are:

- "What is your current role?"
- "What do you enjoy most about your work?"
- "What did you do previously?"
- "Is there anything new in your field that you are excited about?"
- "Is there anything new in your field that you are excited about?"
- "What advice would you give to someone looking to do what you do?"

Be open to talking about yourself by mentioning your skills, projects, or unique experiences that might be valuable to others. As networking is a two-way relationship that you should both view as beneficial, be sure to ask if you can provide any advice, insights, or connections to them. This will help to build goodwill and strengthen your relationships.

As networking is a business relationship rather than a personal one, it should always end with an action plan. Whether it's a follow-up meeting or a recommendation, there should always be a follow-up action.

Be careful not to dominate the conversation to respect each other's time. If the conversation ends early or if there is a schedule change, accept it with grace and exit the meeting with "It was great talking with you. I'll follow up soon!"

Within 24 hours of the meeting, send a follow-up note to thank them for their time and reference something specific you discussed. Also, if not already connected, send a LinkedIn connection request to help build your online network.

Maintain the relationship by following up on any actions agreed upon and keeping the connection alive by checking in, sharing resources, or updating them on your progress.

By being prepared, genuine, and proactive, you can turn face-to-face networking into a rewarding experience that supports your long-term career goals.

ONLINE NETWORKING

Many online job platforms also enable you to connect with other users. Networking on online career platforms can be beneficial for your professional growth and career advancement. It allows you to connect with industry peers, mentors, recruiters, and thought leaders, regardless of location. You can also join professional organizations related to your industry to access exclusive job boards, events, and mentorship opportunities. By using strategic networking opportunities, you can uncover both advertised and hidden opportunities, increasing your chances of success.

Keep your LinkedIn and other online profiles optimized and current to showcase your skills, experience, and career goals. Focus on connecting with people in your industry, alumni from your school, or professionals in roles you aspire to get. When connecting with someone, include a message explaining why you're reaching out (e.g., shared interests, admiration for their work).

Example: "Hi [*name*], I admire your work in [*specific field*]. I'd love to connect and learn more about your experience at [*company*]."

You can also engage with posts, articles, or updates shared by others by adding meaningful comments or insights. Post articles, tips, or achievements that show your expertise and interest in your field. You can also take part in group discussions, or answer questions in forums to increase your visibility.

Attend virtual events, meetups, and panels to meet professionals in your field, and use the chat functions to introduce yourself and follow up with speakers or attendees on LinkedIn afterward.

If you would like to seek a more private meeting with someone, ask for a virtual coffee chat or informational interview to learn about their career path, industry, or company.

Example: "Hi [*name*], I'm exploring career opportunities in [*industry*] and noticed your impressive experience at [*company*]. Would you be open to a brief chat? I'd love to learn from your insights."

If accepted, have thoughtful questions ready to ensure the conversation is valuable for both parties. Remember to give before you ask. Share helpful resources, congratulate others on their achievements, or provide insights where you can. It is important to build a rapport first before asking for favors like job referrals or recommendations.

Maintain relationships by liking their posts, commenting, or sending a message to touch base. If someone helps you, thank them with a message or public acknowledgment on LinkedIn.

EVENT NETWORKING

Networking Events at industry events (such as conferences and seminars) are excellent places to meet professionals in your chosen field, while career fairs often host multiple employers hiring. As for face-to-face networking, planning is key.

Check the guest list if available, familiarize yourself with speakers, panels, and breakout sessions to plan your time, and identify key people you'd like to meet.

Prepare a concise, engaging introduction (30–60 seconds) that explains who you are, what you do, and what you're looking for.

To start conversations with new people, ask a generic question and show genuine interest by listening actively and asking open-ended questions about their work, goals, or challenges. When the conversation turns to you, share relevant insights about your experience or interests while keeping it concise and engaging.

Examples of opening questions

- "What brought you to this event?"
- "Have you attended this before?"

- "What session are you most excited about?"

Dress to reflect industry standards in polished attire appropriate for the event's formality.

Try not to spend all your time with one person but aim to meet several people. Look for groups that appear open to new participants and introduce yourself. If you feel overwhelmed, just step aside to recharge for a short period before re-engaging.

When leaving a conversation, thank the person for their time and ask about staying in touch. Ensure you have their contact details before parting ways.

Example: "It was great talking with you, [name]. I'd love to connect on LinkedIn or stay in touch!"

Within 24 hours, send a follow-up email or LinkedIn message referencing your conversation. Check in, share relevant resources, or comment on their updates periodically to keep the relationship alive.

Example: "Hi [your name], it was a pleasure meeting you at [event name]. I enjoyed our discussion about [topic] and would love to stay connected."

Focus on building rapport rather than pitching your services or asking for favors, and after the event, review your notes and categorize contacts with priority or action items.

By preparing well, engaging, and following up, you can turn event networking into a rewarding experience that helps you grow both professionally and personally.

Networking isn't about immediate results; however, it's about building long-term professional connections. Be genuine in your interactions to foster trust and meaningful relationships. By optimizing your presence, engaging regularly, and focusing on relationship-building, you can network effectively and open doors to new opportunities and collaborations.

Use tools to help with your networking. Follow industry leaders and take part in relevant conversations on online platforms to get noticed by potential employers or join industry-specific associations to access job boards and networking opportunities. There are also networking trackers to keep track of who you've met, their contact information, and follow-up actions.

Overall, networking provides the opportunity to learn about jobs that are not publicly advertised, gain valuable insights about industries, companies, and roles. It can also establish you as a knowledgeable and approachable professional. By adopting strategic networking practices, you can unlock opportunities that go beyond traditional applications and create lasting professional relationships. Whether online or in-person, effective networking is a key component of a successful job hunt.

Example of a Network Tracker

Contact Name	Date of contact	Method of Contact	Company	Notes

ACTIVE LISTENING

In high-pressure environments like networking or interviews, it is easy to get lost in your own thoughts instead of focusing on a conversation, and it is when active listening comes into play.

Active listening is the process of fully concentrating, understanding, responding, and remembering what someone is saying. Unlike passive hearing, active listening requires a focused effort to ensure the speaker feels heard and understood. This skill is essential for effective communication in both personal and professional settings.

When active listening, you are giving the speaker your undivided attention and avoiding or ignoring any distractions like phones or emails. It is important to maintain eye contact with the speaker and use open body language to show engagement.

To help with your understanding of what is being said, focus on comprehending the speaker's message, both verbal and nonverbal. Pay attention to the tone used or emotions expressed and the context of what is being said to grasp the full meaning.

Respond and provide feedback through verbal affirmations ("I see," "That makes sense") during natural breaks in the conversation and nonverbal cues (nodding, smiling) to maintain engagement. In addition, ask clarifying or follow-up questions to show your understanding of the conversation.

Avoid interrupting the speaker by allowing them to finish their thoughts without interjecting. Resist the urge to plan your response while they're still speaking. Instead, keep focusing on what is being said.

To confirm your understanding, summarize or paraphrase the speaker's points ("So, what I hear you saying is that you're concerned about the project deadline.") To help remember the conversation, keep key points for future reference, or act upon them.

Active listening is important because it builds trust by showing the speaker that you value their input and respect their perspective. It helps build relationships as it strengthens connections between you and the speaker, as the speaker feels you understood what they were saying. This doesn't mean that you can't ask questions or clarify points to ensure clear communication and reduce misunderstandings, but that you hear them and understand the speakers' emotions and viewpoints, improving interactions between you.

Practice active listening by eliminating any distractions to create a quiet environment where you can focus on the conversation.

Practice patience by letting the speaker finish their thoughts before responding and use open-ended questions to encourage deeper conversation by asking questions like, "Can you tell me more about that?"

Remember to validate the speaker by acknowledging their feelings or experiences to show empathy and take notes, if appropriate. Jot down key points to stay engaged and remember important details.

By practicing active listening, you can better foster effective communication, create more meaningful connections, and ensure mutual understanding in your conversations.

BUSINESS CARDS

A business card is a compact, professional tool that provides key contact information and serves as a tangible reminder of you and your brand. People still use business cards, and they remain important in professional settings, even in today's digital age. While technology has introduced new ways to exchange contact information, business cards still offer unique advantages that make them relevant and valuable for networking and personal branding. Many cards now include QR codes linking to LinkedIn profiles, websites, or digital portfolios, combining the benefits of physical and digital networking.

While business cards are no longer exchanged in informal or casual networking, or in digital industries, where exchanging digital contact information is more common, in some cultures, people still see the exchange of business cards as a formal business ritual, emphasizing respect and professionalism, and therefore expect them as part of professional etiquette, particularly in formal or traditional settings.

Business Cards allow a quick and reliable way to exchange contact information in a convenient way without the need to rely on devices or internet connectivity. Handing out a business card adds a personal touch to professional encounters and can foster stronger connections, as the other person is also likely to share their business card. Also, having your information available makes it easier for contacts to reach out after a meeting or event. Business cards can also showcase your expertise through the highlighting of certifications, skills, or other offerings.

Because people easily forget brief interactions at busy networking events, a well-designed business card serves as a practical reminder that helps you stand out. A professionally designed card can showcase your attention to detail and reflect your personal or company brand through design, logo, or color scheme, thus acting as a mini advertisement for you or your business.

For an effective business card, include essential information like your name, title, company, phone, email, and website, and if space is available, include elements like a tagline, QR code, or creative design to reflect your brand. The feel of a card can also play a role, so use quality and durable materials for it.

While digital alternatives are growing, the physical nature of

business cards and their ability to create a lasting impression ensure they remain important for many professionals. A well-crafted business card is a timeless investment in your personal and professional brand. People are more likely to keep and revisit business cards compared to quickly exchanged digital details.

THE ELEVATOR PITCH

An elevator pitch is a brief and engaging spoken summary that highlights your identity, your profession, and your aspirations. The idea is to deliver this pitch within 30 to 60 seconds, the same as the duration of a typical elevator ride, although it can last longer than needed. You can use this quick, impactful statement to grab attention, convey value, and leave a memorable impression in various situations, such as networking events, career fairs, and casual encounters.

An elevator pitch should quickly and effectively communicate your professional identity, and highlight your unique skills, achievements, or goals. You should deliver it to spark interest and encourage further conversation. Present it positively, enthusiastically, using clear and simple language. Rehearse the pitch until such time that you can present it naturally and confidently.

Example: "Hi, my name is [*your name*], a [*your job title*] with [*number*] years of experience in [*your industry*]. I specialize in [*your key skill/expertise*], where I've [*briefly describe a significant achievement or responsibility*]. My background includes working with [*mention a notable company or project*], where I [*describe your

contribution or success*]. I am deeply passionate about [*your professional passion/interest*] and offer a distinctive blend of [*your unique skills or traits*] that sets me apart. This allows me to [*explain how your skills benefit others or solve problems*]. I'm excited to explore potential collaborations and share how my expertise can contribute to your organization's success!

An elevator pitch is your opportunity to make a strong first impression. With practice and refinement, you can use it to open doors and build meaningful connections.

THE HANDBILL

A handbill is a concise, one-page document designed to market yourself as a job candidate. While both a handbill and a resume are tools for showcasing your skills and qualifications, they serve distinct purposes and differ in content, tone, and design. A handbill highlights your key skills, qualifications, and career goals in a visually appealing and easily digestible format. Unlike a resume, a handbill is more informal and promotional, serving as a personal "leave-behind" or networking tool.

At networking events, you can share your handbill to make a lasting impression on recruiters and professional contacts. It provides a quick snapshot of your expertise and career goals, avoiding the formality of a resume. A well-designed handbill will help make you stand out. It also serves as a conversation starter during meetings with mentors or industry professionals and guides you in describing your skills and career goals.

Comparing a Handbill and a Resume

Aspect	Handbill	Resume
Length	1 page	1–2 pages
Purpose	Networking and self-promotion	Job applications
Content	Key skills, career highlights, and goals	Detailed work history, education, and skills
Design	Creative and visually engaging	Professional and minimal
Usage	Informal networking events and outreach	Formal job applications

Handbill Content

A handbill should be short and focused and, unlike a resume, often includes professional headshot and professional social media links. The informality of a handbill means you can tailor its content and format to match the industry or audience you're targeting.

A handbill should include your contact information (Name, phone number, email, and LinkedIn profile) and a professional summary that includes a brief statement about your background and career aspirations. Include 5–8 key skills relevant to your target roles, including measurable results or accomplishments that showcase your achievements. You can also highlight your desired level or position by listing the generic job titles. Using generic titles enables it to have a broad appeal. List your career goals by specifying the type of roles, industries, or companies (list 10-15) you're targeting in your job hunt. As a handbill is more informal than a resume, you can include icons, color accents, or a QR code linking to your portfolio or LinkedIn profile.

Elements of a Handbill

Element	Details
Personnel details	Name; phone number, email, and LinkedIn profile
Headshot	Current and Professional
Professional Summary	Highlights of your career to date; skills
Desired Position	List multiple generic titles
Target Companies	List specific companies in the field you wish to work for

A handbill is an excellent tool to use in your job hunt, offering a creative and professional way to market yourself as part of your networking strategy.

WORKING WITH RECRUITERS

Recruiters can play a crucial role in the hiring process, acting as a bridge between candidates and hiring managers. Communicating with recruiters may increase your chances of moving forward in the hiring process and securing the right opportunity.

If the recruiter works for a specific company, learn about the organization, its values, and the role you're pursuing. If they're an independent recruiter or part of a staffing agency, understand their area of specialization and client base.

Define your career goals, preferred roles, industries, and locations before the conversation. Identify the skills, experiences, and achievements you want to highlight.

Treat the recruiter with respect, as they can be your advocate during the hiring process. Explain what you're looking for in your next role, including job titles, industries, and skills you want to use. If you're flexible, mention your willingness to explore different opportunities.

Summarize your career, focusing on achievements and skills relevant to the role. Use the STAR method (Situation, Task, Action, Result) to describe accomplishments, if applicable.

Discuss salary expectations, preferred work environment, and other priorities like remote work, flexibility, or benefits. If you're employed, mention your notice period or availability for interviews.

Respond promptly to emails or calls from the recruiter to show professionalism and commitment and update the recruiter on changes to your availability, interest in the role, or new job offers you may receive.

If a recruiter presents a role to you, inquire about the role and company, ask questions such as "Can you provide more details about the responsibilities and expectations for this position?", "What can you tell me about the company culture and team dynamics?" and "What are the next steps in the hiring process?"

Even if the opportunity doesn't work out, stay professional for future possibilities, and stay in touch and connect with them on LinkedIn to expand your professional network.

By preparing and maintaining a professional and cooperative approach, you can make a powerful impression on recruiters and improve your chances of finding the right opportunity.

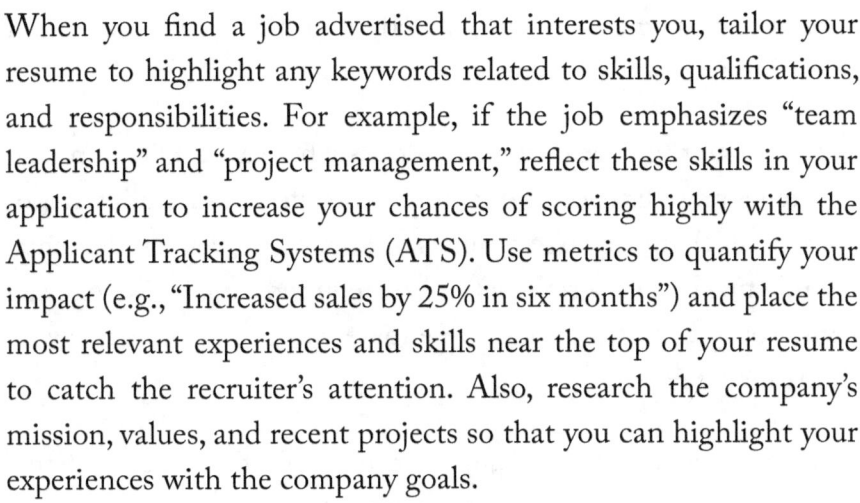

JOB APPLICATIONS

When you find a job advertised that interests you, tailor your resume to highlight any keywords related to skills, qualifications, and responsibilities. For example, if the job emphasizes "team leadership" and "project management," reflect these skills in your application to increase your chances of scoring highly with the Applicant Tracking Systems (ATS). Use metrics to quantify your impact (e.g., "Increased sales by 25% in six months") and place the most relevant experiences and skills near the top of your resume to catch the recruiter's attention. Also, research the company's mission, values, and recent projects so that you can highlight your experiences with the company goals.

COVER LETTER

A cover letter serves as a personalized introduction to your job application. It is an opportunity to provide context to your resume, highlight relevant skills and experiences, and convey enthusiasm for the role and company. It also allows you to clarify aspects of your application, such as employment gaps, career transitions, or relocation intentions.

Always address the letter to the specific hiring manager if their name is available and keep it formal but enthusiastic. Proofread to ensure there are no typos or grammatical errors.

As the application process becomes more automated, remember that many employers still expect cover letters, although their importance varies by industry, company, and job. Cover letters are required if a job description requires one and are often required for positions that require strong communication skills, such as writing, public relations, or management. Also, job applicants should submit letters when applying directly to a hiring manager rather than through an online portal.

A cover letter may be optional for roles where an application process relies on online forms or automated systems or in industries or companies that prioritize resumes or portfolios over supplemental documents. Even if a cover letter isn't required, submitting one can show your extra effort and differentiate you from candidates who didn't include one.

Where an email may be required instead of a formal cover letter, ensure the email includes a clear subject line, such as "Application for [*job title*] - [*your name*]." Briefly introduce yourself and express enthusiasm for the role. Attach your resume and cover letter in PDF format unless otherwise specified.

SUPPLEMENTAL MATERIALS (IF NEEDED)

If applying for creative or technical roles, include a link to a portfolio that showcases your best work. If requested, provide examples of projects or presentations relevant to the role.

REVIEW AND PROOFREAD

For formatting your resume or cover letter, the website, Canva® offers templates and design tools to create visually appealing resumes and cover letters, while Resume Genius™ provides templates and tips for creating effective resumes.

Double-check for typos, grammar mistakes, and formatting inconsistencies. Ask a trusted friend, mentor, or career coach to review your application materials. There are software tools available (Grammarly, Google Docs, ProWritingAid) that can help with proofreading, correcting grammar and spelling errors in your resume, and a cover letter.

Also, when applying, follow all the instructions. Ensure you've included all requested documents and answered any application questions.

TRACK YOUR APPLICATIONS

To help you stay organized, maintain a tracker listing the job title, company name, date applied, and any follow-up notes. Tracking which versions apply to each application helps you reference the correct document during an interview, and seeing your organized efforts can also boost morale.

There are several job tracking and organization tools available for use. Google Sheets and Excel are useful for tracking job applications, interviews, and follow-ups.

Example of a Job Application Tracker

Application Date	Job Title	Company	Recruiter	Response Date	Outcome

By tailoring your applications, you show genuine interest in the role and position yourself as the ideal candidate, increasing your chances of landing an interview.

REFERENCES

References can play a significant role in securing a job, as they provide employers with insights into your skills, character, and work ethic from people who know you professionally. Selecting the right individuals to vouch for you is crucial.

Managers or team leaders you reported to in previous roles can speak to your work performance, leadership skills, and ability to meet goals, while colleagues or coworkers can provide insight into your teamwork, collaboration, and interpersonal skills. Clients or vendors you've worked with in a client or business-facing role can highlight your professionalism and service quality, and recent graduates, mentors, or professors can attest to your skills, work ethic, and character.

When choosing individuals to act as a reference, ensure they can provide specific examples of your achievements and strengths that align with the job you're pursuing. Choose a mix of supervisors, peers, and clients to provide a well-rounded perspective on your abilities. Also, consider selecting references based on the job you are applying for. For example, if you're applying for a leadership role, include someone who can speak to your management skills.

Supervisors or managers can offer insight into your performance and contributions in a professional setting, while colleagues or peers are best at highlighting your teamwork, collaboration, and interpersonal skills. Professors or academic advisors are ideal for academic or research-related opportunities, and mentors or coaches can provide a well-rounded perspective on your personal growth and potential.

Also, avoid anyone with a personal connection (friends and family) as these connections are not credible for professional references. Don't include someone who isn't familiar with your work or may give generic feedback or former employers with negative impressions where your performance or relationship with your manager may have been subpar or contentious.

Avoid selecting people who only know you casually or cannot give detailed feedback about your work. Employers value references who can discuss your most recent work experiences and skills. While long-standing references are valuable, someone who has seen your growth in the last 2–3 years may be more relevant.

Always ask potential references if they're comfortable being contacted and willing to give a positive recommendation before sharing their names with prospective employers. Many companies will contact references as part of their due diligence, so be sure to let your references know about the job, the company, and the skills or experiences you'd like them to emphasize. Inform them they are likely to be contacted and provide details such as the hiring manager's name or company so that they don't miss the call.

Keep in touch with your references even when you're not job searching. Maintaining a positive relationship makes them more willing to help when needed. Show gratitude by thanking them for their support and keeping them updated on your career progress.

It is helpful to maintain a separate list of references so that you are ready to provide them upon request, rather than preemptively including them in your resume. When providing a list of referees to prospective employers, be sure to include the referee's full name, job title, company, email address, and phone number. Add a brief note about your relationship with the referee, such as "Former Manager at [company name] from 2019 to 2021." Choosing the right references can strengthen your application and provide employers with a compelling endorsement of your abilities and character. Select them carefully, prepare them well, and maintain professional relationships to ensure their ongoing support.

When asking for a reference, mention the shared experiences or projects that highlight your connection and their relevance as a reference. However, as not everyone may be comfortable providing a reference for various reasons, be sure to make it easy for the person to decline by acknowledging that you understand if they cannot assist.

Include an offer to share your resume, job descriptions, or other relevant materials to help them craft their responses and end with a sincere thank-you for their time and consideration. This template ensures professionalism, clarity, and respect for the potential reference's time and effort. You may occasionally receive a request for a formal letter of recommendation. This letter is written by someone who has agreed to act as a professional reference for you. Job applications, academic admissions processes, and scholarship submissions may require it.

It is advisable to ask for the letter a minimum of two weeks in advance to allow the writer ample time to compose it. Once completed, send a thank-you note expressing your gratitude for their time and support.

A well-written letter of recommendation can be a powerful tool in strengthening your application and showcasing your potential for success. It can add credibility to your application by offering an external validation of your qualifications and character. It highlights your accomplishments and skills that a resume or application might miss, showing the reader how your skills and attributes meet their needs.

Example Email Reference Request

Subject: Request for Professional Reference

Dear [*Recipient's Name*],

I hope this message finds you well. I'm reaching out to ask if you would kindly serve as a professional reference for me as I apply for [*specific role(s)*].

Having worked together on [*specific project, team, or initiative*], I truly value your insights into my [*specific skills, e.g., "collaborative approach," "problem-solving abilities," or "leadership qualities"*]. I believe your perspective on my work and achievements would provide valuable support to my application.

The potential employers/programs may contact you to discuss my qualifications and professional experience. I will ensure to keep you informed about each opportunity, including sharing the job description or any relevant details so you can tailor your response as needed.

If you're comfortable with this, please let me know, and I would be happy to provide any additional context or materials (e.g., my resume or a summary of the roles I'm targeting) to make the process as easy as possible for you.

Thank you so much for considering this request. I greatly appreciate your time and support, and please let me know if you have any questions or need further information.

Best regards,
[*Your Full Name*]
[*Your Contact Information*]

6

INTERVIEW QUESTIONS

Preparing for an interview is more than just knowing your resume. It's about anticipating the questions and crafting responses that highlight your skills, experience, and value.

From general inquiries about your background to more specific questions about problem-solving or teamwork, these questions assess your qualifications, cultural fit, and ability to thrive in the role. By preparing thoughtful, structured answers using the STAR method (Situation, Task, Action, Result), you'll be able to present yourself as confident, capable, and ready to take on the job.

THE STAR METHOD

The STAR method is a structured approach to answering behavioral interview questions, helping you showcase your skills and experiences. STAR stands for **Situation, Task, Action,** and **Result** and is a framework for responding to questions that ensure your answers are clear, concise, and compelling. This method allows you to tell a story that highlights your qualifications while demonstrating how you've handled challenges or achieved success in the past. Employers often use behavioral questions to help predict future performance, and by using the STAR method, you can provide thoughtful, well-organized responses that leave a lasting impression. Whether you're describing how you led a team, solved a problem, or met a deadline, the STAR method helps you present yourself as a capable and confident candidate.

The four steps of the STAR method are:

1. Situation

Broadly set the scene; where did it happen? When was it? Which company/role, size of the team?

2. Task

Describe the task, problem, or challenge you took responsibility for completing; what was the goal? Major challenges and/or risks, what needed to be done and why.

3. Action

Describe the action(s) that you took to complete the task. Which skills or tools did you use? What were the key decisions made? What obstacles did you overcome?

4. Result

Explain the positive results. What were the results? Did the result tie back to the original goal? Highlight any quantifiable results ($ saved, % improvements, etc.)

WHY THE STAR METHOD

The STAR method is a way to answer behavioral interview questions in an engaging manner. It is effective as it provides responses that are clear and structured, which helps you stay organized and focused, ensuring your answers are logical and easy for the interviewer to follow. Showing: It shows problem-solving skills through a step-by-step breakdown of your approach to challenges, highlighting your ability to identify problems and take initiative. It also allows you to tailor your answers to the specific job requirements by choosing examples that match the skills and attributes that the employer values or by addressing specific qualifications or job expectations.

As the STAR method ends with the result, it emphasizes the measurable impact of your actions and shows how your contributions affected your previous roles or organizations positively. The format allows for simple answers to common interview questions such as, "Can you tell me when…?" which helps interviewers assess your knowledge and abilities. In addition, its repeatable format makes it easy to learn so that you can shape examples in advance, reducing anxiety and ensuring you're ready for the tough questions.

By telling short, relevant stories, you can make your answers stand out more than a rambling or generic response. This shows your ability to communicate effectively.

By using the STAR method, you will provide detailed and results-driven answers that show how you fit the position while building a connection with the interviewer.

EXAMPLES OF THE STAR METHOD

Example Question: "Tell me about yourself"

Example Answer: "I'm a marketing professional with over five years of experience specializing in digital campaigns and brand strategy. Most recently, at [*company name*], I oversaw a multichannel campaign (*Situation*) designed to boost engagement for a new product launch (*Task*). I led a team of three, implementing targeted ads and revamping our social media strategy (*Action*). As a result, the campaign exceeded engagement targets by 25% and increased sales by 15% in the first quarter after launch (*Result*). Before that, I worked at [*previous company*], where I focused on content creation and analytics, which honed my skills in crafting data-driven marketing strategies. I'm excited about this opportunity because your company's emphasis on innovation aligns with my passion for using creativity and analytics to drive results."

Example Question: "Can you tell me about a time when you faced a challenging situation at work and how you handled it?"

Example Answer: "In my previous role as a customer service manager, our team faced a sudden 40% increase in call volume because of a product recall. This led to long waiting times and frustrated customers, which started affecting our satisfaction scores (*Situation*). My task as team leader was to resolve the bottleneck, maintain customer satisfaction, and ensure my team could handle the increased workload without burnout (*Task*). To address the recall, I immediately prioritized common customer concerns, creating a detailed FAQ for agents to resolve calls efficiently using a multistep approach. I reallocated resources by collaborating with other departments to bring in temporary support staff during peak hours. I also enhanced communication by holding daily check-ins with the team to address challenges and provide encouragement, ensuring morale stayed high. Within two weeks, we reduced the average wait time by 50%, and our customer satisfaction scores rebounded to pre-recall levels. The team reported feeling supported and better equipped to handle similar situations in the future (*Result*)."

Example Question: "Describe a mistake you have made?"

Example Answer: "In my previous role as a marketing coordinator, I managed social media campaigns for a new product launch (*Situation*). My responsibilities included creating and scheduling posts across multiple social media platforms to generate excitement and engagement for the product launch (*Task*). In my haste to meet a tight deadline, I overlooked the importance of double-checking the scheduled posts and a post containing incorrect information about the launch date went live. The incorrect post confused our followers, and we received several complaints. I quickly addressed the mistake by posting a correction and issuing an apology (*Action*). This experience taught me the importance of attention to detail and a thorough review. Since then, I've implemented a more rigorous review process to ensure accuracy in all communications (*Result*)."

Example Question: "How do you organize your work?

Example Answer: "In my previous role as a project manager, I oversaw multiple projects with tight deadlines (*Situation*). I ensured all projects met deadlines, budget constraints, and quality standards (*Task*). For: Tracking progress, setting priorities, and allocating resources, I implemented project management software. I also created a detailed project plan, set milestones, and regularly communicated with the team to ensure everyone was on the same page (*Action*). As a result, we completed all projects on time and within budget, and clients gave us positive feedback on our efficient project management (*Result*)."

When answering a question using the STAR method, remember to:

• Tailor your responses to the company and role.

• Practice delivering your answers aloud for clarity and confidence.

• Prepare specific examples that illustrate your experiences and achievements.

To help your preparation, review potential interview questions before you interview and use these questions as a foundation to craft responses that align with your unique career story and ensure you're ready to shine in any interview setting.

Example Interview Questions

Interview Question	Response
Tell Me About Yourself	Describe concisely your past and present jobs; which of your skills and career highlights best fit the role; make them personal and interesting; aim for under 5 mins
Why Are You Interested in This Position?	Identify responsibilities that attract you to the position; specifically, about the impact you could have and how your skills would help

Interview Question	Response
What Are Your Strengths?	Describe skills used successfully in the past that match job description requirements; highlight 2–3 strengths; add stories of times you shined; share how you think these strengths will directly benefit the company
What Are Your Weaknesses?	Describe a trait, and how you manage it or intend to improve it but show how it would not affect your ability to do the job; aim for 1–2 traits.
How Do You Organize Your Work?	Describe how you prioritized your work; delegated, blocked time, and gave frequent updates to management; what techniques you have used to multitask
What Is Your Preferred Leadership Style?	Describe in an honest, short, and positive tone; are you inspiring, team-orientated, supportive, coaching, or focused on results? Are you a bossy or hands-off leader?
Describe A Mistake You Have Made.	Describe an error, actions taken to correct it, and lessons learned; a story of setback, recovered and learned from and moved forward; how would you have handled it with hindsight?
How Do You Handle Workplace Conflict?	Explain in a positive light a situation, action, and outcome when dealing with a conflict.
What Do You Not Like About Your Current Position?	Describe positively how the new position offers the opportunity to further your career
Describe A Challenge You Overcame.	Describe a situation, task, action, and result; how did you adjust and get others on board? How did you solve it and the impact it had?

Interview Question	Response
Describe How You Prioritize Your Work.	Describe how you handled unexpected workload changes; examples where delegated, blocked time, gave updates; techniques used to multitask
Describe How You Handle Stress.	Describe how you deal with stress and how you act to reduce it
What Motivates You?	Describe what in a previous role and the job description of the potential position excites you and how your skills fit
What Do You Bring to The Company?	Describe a skill or experience you have that can help the company; be passionate and excited; show you've done research, mention things you really like
What Has Been Your Greatest Achievement to Date?	Describe a situation, task, and action that resulted in a successful outcome
When Did You Show Leadership?	Describe a situation, task, action, and result that you lead; explain clearly how you solved it/lead a team
What Work Environment Do You Prefer?	Describe in a positive tone, aligning with the company's culture if possible
Why The Change in Career?	Describe honestly and concisely why the change, noting how your experience in the past will help with the current role
Why Are You Looking to Leave Your Current Position?	Describe in an honest, short, and positive tone; highlight the want of a new challenge; improve areas of your skill set; discuss the importance of growth and improvement with new challenges

Additional Interview Questions

1. What do you know about our company?

2. What skills and experiences make you a good fit for this role?

3. What tools or software are you proficient in that apply to this job?

4. What do you hope to achieve in this position?

5. Describe a situation where you had to adapt quickly to a significant change.

6. How do you handle feedback or criticism?

7. Tell me about the time you led a team or project. What was the outcome?

8. How do you plan to contribute to the success of our team?

9. If hired, what would your first 30/60/90 days in this role look like?

10. Demonstrate your understanding of the role and enthusiasm for the opportunity.

11. How do you approach solving complex problems?

12. Have you ever implemented a new idea or process?

13. Tell me about a time you failed and how you handled it.

14. Can you share an example of a goal you set and how you achieved it?

15. Where do you see yourself in five years?

BEHAVIORAL INTERVIEW QUESTIONS

Behavioral questions evaluate how you've handled specific situations in the past to predict future performance. These questions often focus on your problem-solving abilities, interpersonal skills, and decision-making processes.

Positive behavioral questions are used to show what you can bring to the table and so show alignment with the role's requirements. While negative behavioral questions provide insight into your ability to handle adversity, which can be critical in any workplace. Companies use both types of questions to assess your resilience, self-awareness, and ability to grow from experience. Employers often value candidates who can celebrate their wins while also learning and growing from their challenges. A balanced approach to answering both positive and negative behavioral questions is key to presenting yourself as a well-rounded professional.

Positive behavioral questions showcase your strengths, achievements, and competencies and highlight how your actions led to successful outcomes.

Examples:

- "Tell me about a time when you successfully led a team through a challenging project."

- "Can you share an example of a time you exceeded expectations in your role?"

- "Describe a situation where you identified an opportunity for improvement and implemented a solution."

- "Give an example of when you went above and beyond for a client or colleague."

By answering these questions using the STAR Method (Situation, Task, Action, Result) you can emphasize your contributions and the positive impact of your actions and quantify results.

Example Answer: "In my previous role, the team faced a tight deadline on a marketing campaign (*Situation*). As the team leader, I reorganized the project plan, prioritized tasks, and delegated responsibilities based on individual strengths (*Task and Action*). As a result, we delivered the campaign two days early, increasing client engagement by 20% (*Result*)."

Interviewers ask negative behavioral questions to understand how you handle adversity, mistakes, or difficult situations and to assess your self-awareness, problem-solving skills, and ability to learn from experiences.

Examples:

- "Describe a time when you faced conflict with a coworker and how you resolved it."

- "Can you share an example of a mistake you made and how you handled it?"

- "Tell me about a time when you had to deal with a difficult customer."

- "Describe a situation where you failed to meet a goal and what you learned from it."

To answer negative behavioral questions, it is best to focus on the resolution and the lessons learned rather than dwelling on the problem. Avoid blaming others and take responsibility for your actions. Be sure to highlight steps you have taken to improve and prevent similar issues in the future.

Example Answer: "While working on a group project, I initially failed to clarify roles and responsibilities, leading to delays (*Situation*). I took responsibility and quickly scheduled a team meeting to realign tasks and set clearer deadlines (*Task and Action*). From then on, we communicated more effectively and completed the project successfully. This experience taught me the importance of proactive communication (*Result*)."

The best way to answer behavioral questions is to be honest and keep it professional. Provide genuine examples but avoid negative situations that could cast you in a poor light and avoid personal or irrelevant anecdotes; focus on workplace scenarios. Try to prepare your potential answers in advance by reflecting on your experiences and have a mix of positive and negative examples ready. To emphasize your growth, answer negative questions by showing how the experience has made you a stronger professional. Keep your responses focused and under 2 minutes to maintain the interviewer's focus.

Comparison of Positive vs Negative Behavioral Questions

Aspect	Positive Questions	Negative Questions
Focus	Strengths, achievements, and successes	Challenges, conflicts, and mistakes
Purpose	Highlight skills, leadership, and results	Assess resilience, accountability, and growth
Tone	Encouraging and affirming	Reflective and analytical
Response Strategy	Showcase success and quantify impact	Emphasize resolution and lessons learned

SUCCESS STORIES

Success stories are concise narratives that showcase your skills, accomplishments, and ability to deliver results. They are essential for resumes, cover letters, and interviews, when using behavioral frameworks like the STAR method. Well-crafted success stories show your value to employers by providing concrete examples of your achievements.

Reflect on your past roles, volunteer work, or academic projects when identifying success stories. Choose experiences where you solved a problem, achieved significant results, contributed to your team's success, or learned and grew professionally. Tailor your examples to match the job description's skills and qualifications.

Using the STAR method to structure your success stories helps to make them ensure they are clear and effective. Set the context by describing the background or challenge (*Situation*). Then explain your role and the specific responsibility you had (*Task*). Be sure to highlight the steps you took to address the challenge or complete the task (*Action*) and share the outcome, focusing on measurable achievements and the impact you made (*Result*).

Use specific and quantifiable results in your success stories where possible. Include metrics, percentages, or numbers to illustrate your impact, and try to avoid vague statements like "I did well"; instead, focus on tangible outcomes. Highlight your job-relevant skills, such as leadership, problem-solving, or technical expertise, and craft a concise, one-to-two-minute narrative.

Example Success Stories

Example 1: Problem-Solving

- In my previous role as a customer support specialist, because of inefficient processes, the team struggled with long response times (*Situation*). My task was to identify bottlenecks and improve response times. I conducted a workflow analysis, implemented a ticket prioritization system, and trained team members to use new tools (*Action*). This reduced the average response times by 40%, leading to a 20% increase in customer satisfaction ratings (*Result*).

Example 2: Leadership

- As a project manager, my team faced a tight deadline for a high-stakes client project (*Situation*). I had to ensure my team delivered the project on time without compromising quality. I reorganized the project plan, delegated tasks based on team strengths, and implemented daily check-ins to track progress (*Action*). This resulted in the project being delivered two days ahead of schedule, earning a 95% client satisfaction score and securing a follow-up contract worth $250,000 (*Result*).

Example 3: Initiative and Innovation

- In my role as a marketing coordinator, our social media engagement rates were declining (*Situation*). As responsibility for revitalizing our social media strategy was mine (*Task*), I analyzed audience trends, introduced interactive content like polls and Q&A sessions, and leveraged A/B testing to refine our approach (*Action*). This increased engagement rates by 30% within three months and increased the follower base by 15% (*Result*).

You can use success stories on resumes as specific bullet points highlighting accomplishments. Or in cover letters to expand on a success story and show how your experience aligns with the job. In addition, success stories can answer behavioral questions during an interview, for example, "Tell me about a time when you solved a problem". You can also use them to network; sharing your success stories shows your expertise.

Prepare and practice your success stories in advance to ensure you deliver them concisely and confidently, and that you tell them without hesitation. Be sure to keep the success stories positive by focusing on what you accomplished rather than dwelling on challenges or setbacks. Include examples where you learned or adapted, demonstrating resilience and a growth mindset. Always tailor your success stories where applicable.

You should aim for 5 success stories that focus on different areas if possible. By using success stories, you can build your credibility by providing concrete examples of your skills and achievements. Well-told stories are memorable and make you stand out, so try to engage your audience and show your value by highlighting the impact you can have on a potential employer.

By mastering the art of creating and sharing success stories, you can communicate your value and position yourself as the ideal candidate for the role.

ADDRESSING BEING FIRED OR LAID OFF

Addressing being fired or laid off in an interview can be a delicate topic. But it's important to be honest without referring to you or your former employer negatively, as this may reflect poorly on you. It's also best to avoid unnecessary details about the firing, keep the conversation impersonal, and not disclose any confidential information from your previous employer. Employers ask why you left your previous company to determine why you are looking for a new job; was it voluntary or because of performance issues?

When asked, acknowledge the situation without dwelling on it and provide context to help the employer understand the circumstances, but then emphasize your accomplishments, and the skills you developed in your previous role and shift the focus to how you're ready to contribute to the new role.

Contact your former employer or their human resources department, if possible, to understand how they will describe your termination if they receive an inquiry. Aligning your message with theirs and having a clear understanding of their viewpoint will help you provide an accurate account of the situation.

Acknowledge your firing without providing unnecessary details or negative comments about your previous employer. Avoid defensiveness or over-explaining, but acknowledge any relevant mistakes or areas of growth. Focus on what you've done to improve or how the experience has made you a stronger candidate, then redirect the conversation toward your enthusiasm for the new role and how you're better prepared to excel. Even if the termination happened for reasons that may appear unfavorable, being honest shows maturity. You can use gentler language if it helps you feel more comfortable, but ensure you don't leave out any critical details that an employer might uncover during a background or reference check. Always use precise language and avoid saying you were "laid off" if your termination was because of specific behavioral reasons. You don't need to provide every detail, so focus on the facts rather than unnecessary opinions or emotions. After explaining the circumstances, highlight any positive outcomes or steps you've taken to move forward.

Potential employers will want to know what you learned from the experience, if specific behaviors or actions caused your termination. They understand mistakes occur, but what matters most is your ability to learn and use those experiences for self-improvement. Highlight your personal and professional growth by sharing examples of positive changes you've made or how you've learned to handle similar situations in the future.

Redirect the conversation to focus on the skills and attributes that make you an ideal candidate after explaining your termination. Prepare by reviewing the job description and aligning your qualifications with the role's requirements. You can also mention that being let go provided an opportunity to find a position that better matches your skills and values, such as the one you're applying for.

Keep to yourself any negative opinions about your former employer and remain objective about the situation. You want to show the potential employer that you will be a beneficial addition to their team, so speaking ill of past employers may make them question if you will do the same to them. Even if your previous position ended on bad terms, try to focus on the positives of that role. The term "fired" can have negative connotations, so it's best to avoid it while maintaining accuracy. In an interview, your goal is to present yourself as a strong candidate, so use gentler language, like "let go."

Layoffs can occur for a variety of reasons. If applicable, mention that you were part of a larger group that was laid off and, if possible, disclose the number of employees laid off to support this. Outplacement services, if provided, can often help you update your resume, explore new opportunities, and develop new skills. You can then discuss the new skills learned during the interview to illustrate your continued commitment to career development.

It is helpful to have a brief statement prepared that describes why you left your previous job when addressing any separation. This will help you address the question calmly and professionally. During a face-to-face interview, it's important to project confidence, so maintain eye contact, and avoid crossing your arms, which can seem defensive. Demonstrating comfort in discussing the situation can help reassure the potential employer.

For written applications, some employers may ask why you left previous jobs or if you were terminated. Maintain integrity by being truthful in your responses regarding your employment. On the application, keep your responses concise and professional and if applicable, acknowledge the reason for your termination in a neutral, professional way and avoid placing blame on the employer. Instead, highlight what you learned from experience and the steps you've taken to improve. If the application allows for a cover letter, you can use it to highlight your qualifications and address the termination. While you may feel concerned about the impression it might leave, many employers are understanding if you handle the situation appropriately. If the application doesn't ask about termination, focus on your achievements and skills instead of volunteering the information unnecessarily. Then, if your termination comes up during the interview, be ready to provide a consistent, professional explanation and emphasize your growth and how you're better prepared for future roles. Once discussed, redirect the conversation toward your qualifications and enthusiasm for the role.

By addressing the situation with honesty, accountability, and a focus on growth, you can present yourself as a resilient, self-aware, and motivated candidate.

7

INTERVIEW PREPARATION

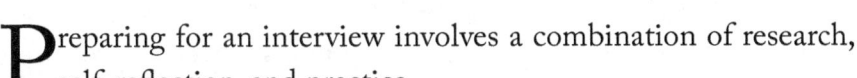

Preparing for an interview involves a combination of research, self-reflection, and practice.

The first step should be to visit the company's website to learn about its goals, culture, and recent achievements. Then familiarize yourself with the company's competitors, challenges, and market position. Review the job description and highlight key responsibilities and requirements to tailor your responses. Be ready to discuss salary expectations, benefits, and availability if the topic arises. Research average salaries for the role to ensure realistic and informed expectations.

Reread your resume to refresh your memory and be ready to discuss every item on your resume, including your skills, experience, and accomplishments, and prepare specific examples of your contributions and successes in previous roles.

You can show your interest in the role and company by asking thoughtful questions, such as:

- "What does success look like in this role?"
- "Can you tell me about the team I'd be working with?"
- For panel: Ask thoughtful questions that address the interests of different panel members.

Be sure to rehearse a confident introduction, including a firm handshake (if in person) with a warm smile, and practice good posture, steady eye contact, and polite responses.

Choose professional attire that aligns with the company's culture and ensure your clothes are clean, pressed, and fit well.

Don't forget to bring extra copies of your resume, a list of references, and a notepad with a pen for taking notes as well as preparing a portfolio or examples of your work, if applicable.

Visualize success and focus on positive outcomes to boost your confidence. Remember to practice deep breathing or mindful exercises to calm your nerves.

In addition, there are online interview preparation tools that can help you practice with peers (Pramp), provide interview questions (Glassdoor), or offer mock interviews (InterviewStream).

When they ask you to attend an interview, research the company and the prospective job position. This knowledge shows genuine interest and helps you tailor your responses to align with the organization's needs.

By preparing, you'll feel confident and ready to make a powerful impression on your potential employer.

RESEARCHING THE COMPANY

While researching a prospective company shows that you're interested and invested in the organization, it also helps you assess whether the company aligns with your values and career goals. Review a company's stated mission or vision and understand the company's purpose or guiding principles to determine what the company offers and how it differentiates itself in the market. It may also be helpful to determine if the company has experienced any recent successes, challenges, changes, or who its competitors are, as these may be useful talking points during the interview. However, be cautious with social media discussions, as they may not provide a complete picture of a company's culture.

RESEARCHING THE ROLE

Read the job description carefully to understand key responsibilities, required skills, and qualifications, and try to match these with your skills and experiences, as this will allow you to tailor your answers to the role. Consider how you might measure success in this role and what potential career paths this position offers.

By researching the company and role team thoroughly, you'll approach the interview with confidence, make a powerful impression, and position yourself as the ideal candidate.

QUESTIONS FOR THE COMPANY

As interviewing is a two-way conversation, you should also have several questions prepared for the interviewer. Asking questions during an interview shows your interest and enthusiasm for the role, helps you evaluate the company, clarifies job expectations and strengthens your connection with the interviewer. Potential questions to ask an interviewer include:

1. How would you describe the company culture?

This helps you understand the work environment and whether it aligns with your values and preferences.

2. What are the company's priorities and goals for the next year?

Shows your interest in the company's direction and how you can contribute to its success.

3. How does the company support professional development and career growth?

Shows your commitment to growth and helps you understand potential opportunities for advancement.

4. What do you enjoy most about working here?

Personal insights can provide a more genuine perspective on the company's strengths and culture.

5. How does the company encourage innovation and adapt to industry changes?

Demonstrates your curiosity about the company's adaptability and long-term vision.

30-60-90 DAY BUSINESS PLANS

A 30-60-90-day business plan structures your goals, strategies, and expected contributions for your first three months in a new role; interviewers, especially those for managerial positions, often request it.

The purpose of a 30-60-90-day plan is to show your strategic thinking and commitment to success. To understand the employer's perspective, if possible, ask the hiring manager or recruiter about success metrics for the role so that you may align your plan with the company's short-term and long-term goals. When defining your goals, focus on three primary areas:

- Learning: Gaining knowledge about the company, industry, and role.
- Performance: Achieving measurable results.
- Integration: Building relationships and becoming part of the team.

Divide your plan into three sections: 30, 60, and 90 days, and tailor the plan to the role and company, rather than using a generic template, to show how your plan supports the organization's priorities and values.

Acknowledge that priorities may shift as you gain more information about the role. Be prepared to justify why you have included specific goals or strategies and frame the plan as a partnership tool rather than a rigid checklist. By preparing a thoughtful, tailored 30-60-90-day plan, you show your ability to hit the ground running, adapt to new environments and contribute meaningfully to your new role.

Example 30-60-90 Day Plan Format

Day Range	Aim	Activities	Deliverables
1–30 Understand the organization, team, and role	Learn & observe	Attend onboarding and training sessions. Review company processes, tools, and resources. Meet with team members and key stakeholders to understand priorities and expectations. Identify immediate challenges and opportunities.	A summary of what you've learned. A list of prioritized goals based on initial observations.
31–60 Begin making meaningful contributions and refining strategies	Plan & contribute	Apply what you've learned to complete tasks and tackle initial challenges. Develop detailed plans for ongoing projects or initiatives. Seek feedback on your performance and adjust accordingly. Strengthen relationships with colleagues and stakeholders	Progress reports on key projects. Refined goals based on insights gained in the first 30 days

Day Range	Aim	Activities	Deliverables
61–90 The 90-Day Phase: Performing and Innovating	Perform & deliver	Implement strategies to meet or exceed performance targets. Propose process improvements or innovative solutions to challenges. Build a sound foundation for long-term success	Completed projects or significant milestones. A roadmap for future contributions

DRESSING FOR SUCCESS

Your attire for an interview plays a crucial role in creating a positive first impression. Dressing appropriately shows your professionalism, respect for the opportunity, and the company.

While a company may present itself with a relaxed atmosphere, it is always better to be over-dressed than under-dressed for an interview. Unless the company hiring representative or recruiter states otherwise, neat and professional attire sends the message that you are serious about the position and respect the interview process.

It is always better to dress professionally for an interview. This does not mean you can't show individuality, but you should avoid overly trendy or distracting clothing by staying with a classic, polished look. In addition, ensure your outfit is clean, well-fitted, and free of wrinkles. It is also best to avoid strong fragrances, as some people may be sensitive to smells. If possible, carry water, tissues, or mints for in-person interviews.

Another factor to keep in mind is comfort. An interview is stressful enough without having to worry about your clothing, so prioritize clothing that is comfortable and that you feel confident wearing.

Consider using a simple bag or portfolio to carry your most recently updated resume. If a presentation is required, prepare for IT issues and bring a printed and a USB copy of your presentation.

Dress Examples

Corporate/Business Formal Environments	
Men	A tailored suit in neutral colors (black, navy, gray); long-sleeve dress shirt, conservative tie, polished dress shoes and dark socks
Women	A pantsuit, skirt suit, or tailored dress in neutral colors, closed-toe heels or flats with minimal and professional jewelry.
Business Casual Environments	
Men	Dress slacks or chinos and a collared shirt (button-up or polo), blazer is optional but adds a professional touch, Leather loafers or Oxfords.
Women	A blouse with dress pants or a modest skirt., cardigan or blazer for added professionalism with comfortable flats or low heels
Virtual Interviews	
Dress professionally from head to toe to maintain the right mindset and avoid surprises if you need to stand up.	
Avoid patterns or colors that clash with your background or appear distracting on camera.	

BODY LANGUAGE

Nonverbal communication often speaks louder than words, with first impressions based on your body language, tone of voice, and then the words that you use. Maintaining appropriate posture during an interview conveys confidence, professionalism, and engagement, creating a strong and positive impression because strong posture often shows self-assurance and readiness.

To convey confidence when entering a room, stand tall and walk with a straight back and relaxed shoulders. When greeting someone, offer a firm but not overpowering handshake while maintaining eye contact and a warm smile.

To avoid appearing disinterested or unprofessional, sit up straight with your back aligned to the chair's back when seated and not slouch. A slight forward lean shows interest and attentiveness but doesn't invade the interviewer's personal space. Place your feet flat on the floor or cross them at the ankles to avoid excessive movement or fidgeting.

Rest your hands on your lap or the table and use them naturally to emphasize points during the conversation. Keep an open and approachable posture and try not to cross your arms, as this can make you appear defensive or closed off.

Look at the interviewer when they're speaking to show engagement, but remember to look away every so often, so you don't end up staring. Attentive posture shows interest in the conversation and respect for the interviewer.

Occasionally, nod your head slightly to acknowledge that you are listening to the conversation and that you understand. This is better than verbally acknowledging the conversation, which can appear as an interruption. Looking down too much can make you seem defensive and untrustworthy.

Avoid tapping your fingers, bouncing your legs, or playing with objects like pens or jewelry, as this can be a distraction. Keep your gestures natural but try to minimize them to avoid showing your nervous energy, instead of presenting a calm and professional demeanor.

While subtly mirroring the interviewer's expressions can create a sense of connection, if you don't overdo it, nothing beats a warm, natural smile which can help build rapport and convey enthusiasm for the role.

When the interview has ended, rise from your chair smoothly and thank the interviewer with a positive demeanor while maintaining eye contact. A firm handshake paired with a smile will also reinforce your professionalism.

Practicing good posture can help you feel more in control and calm during the interview. By maintaining an appropriate body posture, you can project professionalism, enthusiasm, and confidence, helping you leave a lasting positive impression.

PLAN YOUR LOGISTICS

Planning the logistics of your interview ensures you're prepared, punctual, and calm on the big day. Save the recruiter's or interviewer's phone number in case of delays or emergencies. Charge your phone, laptop, or tablet, and bring a portable charger if needed.

Confirm the time, time zone if needed, and date. To be flexible, avoid scheduling any commitments right before or after the interview to give yourself time to focus and regroup.

If it's an in-person interview, confirm the exact address, building, and room number and aim to arrive 10–15 minutes early to settle yourself without feeling rushed. Determine the best route and estimated travel time accounting for traffic or public transit delays. If driving, research parking options near the interview location and carry cash or a card for parking fees.

Know the interview format (e.g., in-person, virtual, or phone), but be prepared for last-minute changes. They may ask you to join a group for lunch; treat this like a panel interview. A scheduling change might switch an in-person interview to a virtual one, or a virtual interview might become a virtual panel interview.

For virtual interviews, confirm the platform (e.g., Zoom, Microsoft Teams, etc.) and link. Test your technology if it's a virtual interview, checking your camera, microphone, and internet connection in advance. Find a distraction-free, well-lit area with a neutral background and plan to join the meeting 5 to 10 minutes before the scheduled time to address any last-minute issues. For back-to-back interviews, ensure you have water and snacks available to have in between interviews.

Finally, prepare alternatives in case of travel delays, technical issues, or last-minute changes. By planning the logistics of your interview, you can help reduce the stress of the interview.

PRE-INTERVIEW NERVES

Job interview anxiety is common, even for experienced professionals. The key to managing it is preparation, mindset shifts, and practical strategies.

Being prepared can help calm your nerves, so ensure you have researched the company and role and practice the common interview questions. Some people find conducting mock interviews with a friend, mentor or coach can help with the anxiety as it simulates the interview experience.

Focus on what you can control, so plan your logistics by confirming the interview time, location, or platform (for virtual interviews) to avoid last-minute stress. If the interview is virtual, test your technology beforehand (headset, microphone connection, camera). Prepare all your materials (resume, notebook, pen, etc.) in advance and dress comfortably and professionally.

Remember that interviews are a two-way conversation. It is as much as you are interviewing them as they are interviewing you, and remind yourself that getting an interview is an achievement. Also, no one expects you to be perfect, so if you stumble, take a breath, correct yourself, and move on confidently.

To help control your nerves before the interview, practice deep, slow breaths to calm your body and mind. Try inhaling for four counts, holding for four counts, and exhaling for six counts. Tense and release different muscle groups to reduce physical tension. Picture yourself succeeding in the interview, answering questions confidently, and building rapport with the interviewer.

Remember that feeling nervous is normal, and that everyone goes through this. Each interview improves your skills and prepares you for future opportunities. Rest well the night before to ensure mental clarity and avoid heavy or sugary foods before the interview to stay energized and focused.

By adopting these strategies, you can manage your anxiety and face interviews with confidence and clarity, enhancing your chances of success.

Your resume alone initially shapes the interviewers' and interviewees' opinions because they rarely know each other. As they invited you for an interview based on your resume, then you can assume that they already think you may be a good match for the role. As a result, an interview then becomes confirmation that you do indeed have the qualifications noted in your resume, so you are halfway there!

8

INTERVIEW DAY

From the moment you arrive at the location of the interview, address everyone respectfully, including receptionists or assistants, as you don't know who may see you.

When the interview is in person, arrive 10 to 15 minutes early (connect 5 to 10 minutes early, if virtual) to show your reliability and respect for the interviewer's time. Greet the interviewer with a firm handshake (if in person) and a warm smile. Maintain good posture and steady eye contact throughout and speak clearly during the interview.

Pay close attention to the questions being asked and try not to interrupt, so that you can answer appropriately. Speak clearly and confidently, remaining approachable and respectful. If multiple questions come at once, prioritize answering one question before moving to the next. Avoid questions about salary or benefits unless the interviewer brings them up.

Ask for clarification if a question is unclear and if you don't know an answer, stay calm and say, "That's a great question; let me think about it for a moment." If you make a mistake, acknowledge it and move on confidently.

By acting professionally, staying calm under pressure, and showing genuine interest, you'll leave a lasting positive impression that sets you apart from other candidates.

ENDING AN INTERVIEW

Ending an interview on a strong and professional note is just as important as your performance during it.

Thank the interviewer for their time and the opportunity to discuss the role.

Example: "Thank you so much for taking the time to speak with me today. I appreciate learning more about the role and the company."

Follow by reaffirming your interest in the role by letting the interviewer know.

Example: "I'm very excited about the opportunity to contribute to your team and feel that my skills align well with the needs of the position."

Inquire about the next steps in the interview process so that you are ready for any follow-up.

Example: "Could you share what the next steps in the hiring process might be?"

Ask if they have any concerns about you so that you can address them at that time.

Example: "Do you have any concerns about my ability to step successfully into this role?"

Ask if they need any additional information from you.

Example: "Is there anything else I can provide to help with your decision?"

Close the interview with confidence, gratitude, and professionalism, so that you leave a positive and lasting impression.

Example: "Thank you again for this wonderful opportunity. I look forward to hearing from you soon."

Remember to maintain a professional posture and attitude until you have left the vicinity of the building (or the virtual meeting has ended).

Within 24 hours, send a personal thank-you email that expresses your gratitude again for the opportunity, reaffirms your enthusiasm for the role, and refers to a specific topic from the interview to make it personal.

TALENT ACQUISITION REPRESENTATIVES

Your first interaction with a company is likely to be with a talent acquisition representative. These are employees of a company responsible for finding, attracting, and hiring the best candidates for job positions within an organization and often acting as a gatekeeper to the company. Their role is crucial in building a skilled and effective workforce, and often they will be your point of contact during the interview process.

The primary responsibilities of a talent acquisition representative include marketing the open position by writing and posting job advertisements on various platforms to attract potential candidates. They are often the people who identify candidates, review resumes, and reach out to potential candidates through various channels, such as social media, job boards, and networking events.

During the interview process, they may conduct the initial interviews to assess an interviewee's skills, experience, and fit for the role. If they think you will be a good fit, they will then schedule and coordinate interviews between interviewees and the hiring managers. A talent acquisition representative may also act as the candidate relationship manager, maintaining communication with all candidates throughout the hiring process to ensure a smooth and positive experience for those being interviewed. Other responsibilities they may have include employer branding, whereby they promote the company as an attractive place to work. They may also provide data analysis on the hiring process, by analyzing hiring data and metrics to improve the recruitment process.

A talent acquisition representative plays a pivotal role in ensuring that the organization attracts top talent, which is essential for its success and growth. Their interactions with you and their input can often be a deciding factor between closely ranked candidates.

Because of their pivotal role in the hiring process, interactions with them are a crucial part of the application process. As such, always maintain a professional tone in your communications and interact with them as you would with a hiring manager.

During interactions, use proper greetings and pay attention to grammar and spelling. Be ready to discuss your qualifications, experiences, and why you're interested in the role, and when responding to questions, be clear and to the point, providing specific examples to back up your claims. Also, remember to express your enthusiasm for the role and the company as genuine interest can set you apart from other candidates. Prepare a few thoughtful questions about the role, company culture, and team to show that you're engaged and interested in the opportunity. After your interaction, send a thank-you email expressing your appreciation for the opportunity to discuss the role and to reinforce your interest and professionalism.

By leaving a positive impression with the talent acquisition representative, you may increase your chances of moving forward in the hiring process.

TELEPHONE INTERVIEWS

Telephone interviews are often the first step in the hiring process, used to screen candidates before moving to more detailed discussions.

While phone interviews are often planned, it can also be the case where the recruiter or talent acquisition representative from a company will call you directly unannounced. Although you might want to send them to voicemail, always answer the call to avoid missing the opportunity.

If you are not ready or able to take a call, then politely explain the situation and ask to reschedule for a time that is convenient for both.

Example: "Thank you so much for reaching out. I appreciate the opportunity to speak with you. Unfortunately, I'm not available at the moment. Could we possibly reschedule our call for [*suggested date and time*], or is there another time that works better for you? I look forward to discussing the opportunity further."

Alternatively, in the event you don't recall the details of the job application being discussed, then politely ask for a reminder.

Example: "Thank you for reaching out. I appreciate your call. Unfortunately, I don't have my application materials in front of me at the moment. Could you please remind me of the position you're referring to? I'd be happy to discuss it further. Alternatively, if you prefer, we can reschedule this call for a time when I can be more prepared. When would be convenient for you? Thank you for your understanding. I look forward to speaking with you."

For planned telephone interviews, ensure you choose a location to take the call that is free from noise and interruptions so that both parties can focus on the conversation. Avoid multitasking, as even slight distractions can affect the quality of your responses.

While phone interviews share similarities with video interviews, the lack of visual cues requires some adjustments to how you prepare and communicate. Since the interviewer can't see you, be precise and vivid in describing your experiences.

You should focus on your voice and tone to provide the best impression to the other person. Speak slowly and avoid mumbling to ensure you're easily understood. Use varied tones to convey interest and confidence, and smile while talking. Smiling while speaking makes your tone sound more positive and engaging. Always give the interviewer time to finish speaking before answering to ensure you hear the complete questions. Use verbal cues like "That's a great question" to show attentiveness or politely ask for clarification if a question isn't clear.

Unlike video or in-person interviews, phone interviews allow you to use notes without being seen. However, to avoid using monotone speech, do not read any written responses. Instead, prepare a list of bullet points about your qualifications and key talking points. Also, highlight keywords or responsibilities related to the job description to reference during the call.

Always prepare the same as you would for any other type of interview by researching the role and company, reminding yourself of the job description and your resume, and preparing for questions to be asked and for you to ask. Within 24 hours, send a thank-you email to express your gratitude for the opportunity and to reaffirm your enthusiasm for the position.

When applying for jobs, always ensure that you have charged your phone, that it has good reception, and that it works, as you never know when a call might arrive.

VIRTUAL INTERVIEWS

Virtual interviews have become a standard part of the hiring process. They allow a company to widen the area of potential candidates without incurring additional up-front costs in the initial interview process. Often companies will only schedule a face-to-face interview once they have narrowed down the selection to only 2 to 3 candidates. Virtual interviews save money and shorten the hiring process by easily accommodating everyone's schedules.

While like in-person interviews, they require unique preparations to ensure a smooth and professional experience, it's helpful to conduct a mock interview with a friend or mentor to gain confidence with the format.

Ensure your computer, webcam, microphone, and internet connection are functioning. Familiarize yourself with platforms like Zoom, Microsoft Teams, or Google Meet. Test logging in and using features like screen sharing. Always have a secondary device or phone number ready; this allows the interview to proceed if unforeseen technical issues arise.

To limit any interruptions or disturbances, find a private location. Inform others in your household of your interview and remove pets where possible to minimize disturbances. Don't forget to silence your phone and disable notifications on your computer to remove these distractions as well.

A tidy, neutral background is best, and when interviewing for remote positions, the background can be a good way to showcase the professional environment of your work-from-home (WFH) office. Alternatively, many platforms allow you to choose a virtual background.

Another consideration is lighting. Use front-facing lighting, so your face is well-lit by natural light, or a lamp placed in front of you so that the interviewer can see you.

Keep your resume, job description, and any notes nearby for easy reference. However, any notes available should be just as reminders. Don't read your notes as the interviewer will note this.

Ensure you have a pen and paper on hand for jotting down important points and a glass of water is helpful in case your throat gets dry. Also, remove any items that could make additional noise during the interview process.

Log in 5–10 minutes early to show professionalism and account for any last-minute issues. Look directly at the camera, not the screen, to simulate eye contact, as this creates a stronger connection with the interviewer. Also, adjust the camera to ensure your head and shoulders are clearly visible and not cut off or hidden.

Speak clearly to avoid miscommunication and pause before responding to ensure the interviewer has finished speaking before you reply to avoid talking over them because of lag.

Sit up straight and maintain a positive, engaged demeanor. If something goes wrong, remain calm and professional and say, "It seems there's a technical issue; let me try to fix it." Reconnect as quickly as possible and apologize for the disruption.

Some companies may work with specific virtual video platforms (myInterview, Jobma, SparkHire) to facilitate the interview process. In addition, these platforms may offer one-way (asynchronous) video interviews.

By preparing thoroughly and approaching the virtual interview with professionalism, you can create a strong impression and increase your chances of success.

ONE-WAY VIDEO INTERVIEWS

A one-way (asynchronous) video interview, also known as an asynchronous video interview, is a modern interviewing method where candidates record their responses to a set of predefined questions without a live interviewer present. This allows employers to interview multiple candidates, ensure all candidates have the same experience, and answer the same questions. This ensures a consistent hiring process between candidates and enables the hiring team to review responses on their schedule. While for candidates it allows them to complete the interview at a time and location convenient for them and provides an opportunity to prepare answers but still record responses within the time frame.

For these types of interviews, you will receive an invitation via an email that includes a link to the interview platform. The interview platform will then provide instructions and guidelines on how to complete the interview, including any technical requirements. The interview platform then presents candidates with a series of questions, which may be text-based or pre-recorded by the employer. Candidates must record their answers using a webcam or smartphone camera within a specified time limit for each question. Most times, you will have the opportunity to review and re-record your response before submitting it. After recording all responses, candidates submit the interview for the hiring team's review at their convenience.

Overall, one-way video interviews offer a convenient and efficient way for both employers and candidates to engage in the initial stages of the hiring process.

PANEL INTERVIEWS

A panel interview involves multiple interviewers interviewing one applicant at the same time and can feel more challenging than a one-on-one interview.

If you receive advance notification of a panel interview, request the names, roles, and departments of the panel members from the recruiter or company talent acquisition representative. As each panelist may focus on specific aspects of your qualifications, such as technical skills, teamwork, or cultural fit, it may be helpful to know their respective perspectives. In addition, bring in enough copies of your resume or portfolio for all panelists to reference during the interview.

Expect diverse questions during a panel interview, since panelists often represent different interests within the company. This is where the prior research of the company may help to showcase your in-depth understanding of the company and your role in addressing each panelist's individual concerns.

When you first enter the room, greet each panelist individually with eye contact, a smile, and a handshake (if in person). If provided, arrange business cards in panelist order to aid name recognition and enable appropriate addressing during the discussion.

Make eye contact with the person asking the question, then briefly glance at other panelists to keep everyone engaged. If possible, avoid focusing on one person so as not to exclude anyone from the conversation.

FORMAL INTERVIEW PRESENTATIONS

Some companies may require a presentation during the interview process. To make a lasting positive impression, practice your presentation skills multiple times beforehand to familiarize yourself with your material and timing. Recording yourself or presenting to a friend for feedback on clarity, pacing, and delivery can be very helpful as well.

Understand who you're speaking to and tailor your content to their interests, knowledge level, and goals. This will also allow you to anticipate questions they might have and to be clear about the goal of your presentation. If needed, ask the recruiter or hiring representative to gain more insight into the purpose of the presentation or to ask any clarifying questions.

You can divide most presentations into three sections: the introduction, the body, and the conclusion. The introduction should start with a strong opening to grab attention and introduce your topic. During the main section of the presentation, present key points, using evidence or examples to support them. In conclusion, summarize your main points and end with a call to action or memorable closing.

Use slides, charts, or props to enhance understanding, but keep them simple and uncluttered. Follow the "6x6 rule" for slides: No more than six words per line and six lines per slide.

To engage your audience, it's helpful to start with a story, question, or statistics to hook your audience and help ease you into the presentation. Remember to look at individuals or your webcam (for virtual presentations) to create a connection. Speak clearly and vary your voice tone and pace to keep your audience engaged. Practice deep breathing to stay calm before and during your presentation.

Remember that slight nervousness is normal. Stand or sit up straight and use natural gestures to emphasize points. Avoid fidgeting or crossing your arms, which can convey nervousness or defensiveness. Familiarity with your material builds confidence and reduces anxiety. Arrive early to test equipment and get comfortable with the space. Instead of focusing on your fear, concentrate on delivering value to your audience, encourage questions, and listen before responding. If you don't know an answer, admit it and offer to follow up later.

INTERNAL INTERVIEWS

Interviewing for a new role within your current company comes with unique advantages and challenges. While you may already be familiar with the organization, it's still crucial to prepare to showcase your readiness for the new opportunity. Prepare as thoroughly as you would for an external position. Avoid assuming the interview will be informal or easy just because you're an internal candidate.

Review the job description to understand the responsibilities, required skills, and success metrics, to align your experience and achievements with the demands of the role. Be ready to explain why you want the new role and how your skills align with its requirements. Learn about the culture, priorities, and challenges of the team you're hoping to join and speak with colleagues who work in the department to gain insights.

Prepare specific examples of how you've contributed to the company's success, using the STAR method (Situation, Task, Action, Result) to describe your accomplishments and highlight your skills and experiences that show your readiness to take on new challenges. Share how you've grown in your current role and how those lessons prepare you for the next step.

Speak with self-assurance about your achievements, but temper it to avoid sounding arrogant. Acknowledge areas where you hope to grow and explain how the new role supports that growth. Ask insightful questions about the role, team goals, and expectations. Finally, be prepared to discuss how you'll ensure a smooth transfer of responsibilities in your current role, suggesting ways to help the company manage the transition.

To show that you've thought about how you can contribute to the new position, highlight collaborations with other teams to show your ability to work across the organization. While acknowledging your contributions in your current role, emphasize how you'll bring value to the new position. Also, be ready to show your understanding of the company's goals and vision, reflecting on how your work aligns with the organization's mission and values.

If selected, maintain professionalism as you transition to the new role. If not selected, request feedback to understand areas for growth and remain committed to excelling in your current position. Use the insights gained during the interview process to identify skills or knowledge to develop further.

By preparing and approaching the process with professionalism and humility, you'll maximize your chances of making a strong impression and securing the internal role.

9

INTERVIEW FOLLOW-UP

Following up after an interview is a critical step in the job application process. It shows professionalism, enthusiasm, and your interest in the role.

Within 24 hours, send a personal thank-you email to each interviewer for their time and the opportunity to discuss the role. Reference a specific topic from the interview to make it personal and reiterate your interest in the role and the company. Let them know you're happy to provide any further details and close with a professional sign-off. If you do not have an email address for each interviewer, you can also send a polite connection request with a note thanking them for the interview.

If you have not heard within the timeframe mentioned during the interview (usually 1-2 weeks), it is appropriate to send an email to check on the status of the hiring decision. In the follow-up email, be polite and acknowledge their busy schedule. Gently inquire about the status of your application and show an understanding of the process.

If you don't hear after 1 to 2 follow-ups, consider the process concluded and move forward with your job search.

EXAMPLE THANK-YOU EMAIL

Subject: Thank You for the Opportunity

Dear [*Interviewer's Name*],

I hope this message finds you well. Thank you for the chance to interview for the [*job title*] position at [*company name*] on [*interview date*]. I enjoyed learning more about the role of your team, and the exciting work being done at [*company name*].

Our conversation about [*specific topic discussed during the interview*] was particularly insightful, and it has only increased my enthusiasm for joining your team. I'm confident my skills in [*specific skills relevant to the role*] and my experience in [*relevant experience*] would allow me to contribute meaningfully to your goals.

Please don't hesitate to reach out if you need any additional information from my side. Thank you once again for your time and consideration. I look forward to the possibility of contributing to [*company name*]'s success.

Best regards,

[*Your Full Name*]
[*Your Contact Information*]
[*Optional: LinkedIn Profile or Portfolio Link*]

EXAMPLE FOLLOW-UP EMAIL

Subject: Follow-Up on [*Position Name*] Interview

Dear [*Interviewer's Name*],

I hope this email finds you well. I'm following up on my application for the [*position name*] role. During our discussion on [*date of interview*], I really enjoyed gaining insights into [*specific details discussed, e.g., the team's innovative projects or the company's culture*].

I'm excited about the opportunity to support [*specific goal or value of the company, e.g., "driving growth in your marketing initiatives"*] and am eager to bring my skills in [*specific skills related to the role*] to your team.

If there's any additional information I can provide or if you need further details to assist in your decision-making process, please don't hesitate to reach out. I appreciate the time you and the team have already dedicated to considering my application.

Thank you for your time and consideration. I look forward to hearing from you soon.

Best regards,

[*Your Full Name*]
[*Your Contact Information*]
[*Optional: LinkedIn Profile or Portfolio Link*]

EXAMPLE THANK-YOU LETTER

[*Your Name*]
[*Your Address*]
[*City, State, ZIP Code*]
[*Your Email Address*]
[*Your Phone Number*]
[*Date*]

[*Hiring Manager's Name*]
[*Company Name*]
[*Company Address*]
[*City, State, ZIP Code*]

Subject: Follow-Up on [*Position Name*] Interview

Dear [*Interviewer's Name*],

I wanted to thank you for the opportunity to interview for the [*job title*] position at [*company name*] on [*date*]. I enjoyed our conversation and learning more about the exciting work being done at [*specific department or team*].

Our discussion about [*specific topic discussed, e.g., "the upcoming project on X" or "your team's collaborative approach"*] reinforced my enthusiasm for joining your team. I'm positive that my skills in [*specific skills or experiences relevant to the role*] would enable me to make meaningful contributions to [*specific company goal or project*].

If there's any additional information I can provide or further steps you'd like me to take, please don't hesitate to let me know. Thank you again for the insightful discussion and for considering my application. I look forward to the possibility of contributing to [*company name*]'s success.

Best regards,
[*Your Full Name*]
[*Your Contact Information*]
[*Optional: LinkedIn Profile or Portfolio Link*]

EXAMPLE FOLLOW-UP LETTER

[*Your Name*]
[*Your Address*]
[*City, State, ZIP Code*]
[*Your Email Address*]
[*Your Phone Number*]
[*Date*]

[*Hiring Manager's Name*]
[*Company Name*]
[*Company Address*]
[*City, State, ZIP Code*]

Subject: Follow-Up on [*Position Name*] Interview

Dear [*Interviewer's Name*],

Concerning: I'd like to inquire about the status of my application for the [*position name*] position. I enjoyed our conversation on [*interview date*] and learning more about [*specific details about the role discussed during the interview*].

The opportunity to contribute to [*specific company goal or project*] excites me, and my [*relevant skills or experiences*] are well-suited to your team's needs.

I understand the hiring process can take time, and I appreciate the opportunity to be considered. Please let me know if there are any updates on the next steps, or if you need anything further from me.

Thank you once again for the opportunity. I look forward to hearing from you and hope to contribute to the exciting work at [*company name*].

Best regards,

[*Your Full Name*]
[*Your Contact Information*]
[*Optional: LinkedIn Profile or Portfolio Link*]

TRACKING APPLICATIONS

Tracking the job applications you have submitted is a crucial step in maintaining organization, evaluating progress, and identifying areas for improvement during your job search.

It helps prevent confusion about which jobs you've applied for, helping you to avoid applying to the same position twice or using the wrong job title and helping to avoid any missed opportunities. It also allows you to prepare for follow-ups, as it can provide a clear overview of where you stand in the application process for each role so that you can ensure timely follow-ups with potential employers, demonstrating enthusiasm and professionalism.

A tracker will also help keep you motivated as you can follow your progress and identify any potential patterns in your success. It can also provide insight into how many applications you've submitted over a period and help you keep a record of important dates, such as application deadlines or interview schedules.

Tracking applications help to remind you of your effort and progress so that you can stay organized, focused, and strategic in your job search efforts, keeping you motivated during the job search process. It also provides you with the opportunity to reflect on what works and what doesn't, enabling you to refine your approach.

There are various ways that you can track your applications, from using a dedicated notebook, spreadsheets, or online tools such as Trello or dedicated job-search-specific tools like JibberJobber and Huntr.

It is beneficial to reflect periodically on your progress, as this can help you determine which types of jobs or industries are yielding the most interviews or find that certain networking strategies or application methods are more effective. This will help you identify areas for improvement, such as whether your resumes or cover letters fail to generate responses or whether you could improve your interview skills based on feedback or self-assessment.

For example, if after reviewing, you notice you've sent 20 applications, but most responses are from roles where you customized your resume. You can assume personalized applications seem more effective than generic submissions. As a result, you should then dedicate more time to tailor applications, even if it means applying for fewer jobs.

View any rejections as a learning experience. If you receive feedback from rejections, analyze the reasons for the rejection and address any gaps you can. You can also reflect on whether the roles you applied for aligned well with your current skills and goals. As you learn more about your job hunt, you can change your strategy based on these insights, perhaps by targeting new industries, enhancing skills, or refining your brand. Reviewing your approach ensures that your job hunt becomes more effective.

Suggested Items to Track

ACTIVITY	ITEMS TO TRACK
Applications Submitted	• Job Title, company name, and location • Date of application and submission method (e.g., job board, company website, referral) • Status (e.g., under review, interview scheduled, rejected)
Networking Efforts	• Names of contacts, their roles, and companies • Date and method of interaction (e.g., LinkedIn message, coffee meeting) • Notes on discussions and any follow-up needed
Interviews	• Date, time, and location (or virtual link) of the interview • Names of interviewers and their roles • Key takeaways, questions asked, and areas for improvement
Follow-Ups	• Dates and content of thank-you emails or messages • Responses received, and the next steps indicated by the employer
Results	• Offers received, terms negotiated, and outcomes • Reasons for rejection, if provided, to identify trends or gaps

REFLECTIONS

Taking notes on the topics that were discussed during an interview and documenting follow-up actions is a key part of maintaining professionalism and maximizing your chances of success in the hiring process.

Interviews can be fast-paced, and it's easy to forget specifics after time has passed, so recording details ensures you remember key points about the role, expectations, and company culture. It can also help you recall deadlines, tasks (e.g., submitting additional materials), or future interview dates.

Referring to specific topics discussed during the interview in your thank-you email shows attention to detail and genuine interest. Mentioning follow-up actions, such as clarifying a question or submitting additional documents, reinforces your enthusiasm and reliability.

Reviewing your notes allows you to evaluate whether the company, role, and team align with your career goals and preferences. When considering multiple opportunities, your notes can provide a basis for comparing roles, enabling you to make informed decisions.

If there are multiple interview rounds, your notes may help you build on previous discussions and avoid repeating information. You can then expect follow-up questions or areas of focus by knowing what earlier interviews emphasized.

Notes may also allow you to reflect on your responses, identify strengths, and recognize areas for improvement. Identifying recurring questions or themes can help you better prepare for future interviews. In addition, recording the names, roles, and contact information of interviewers makes it easier to follow up or connect after the interview. This will then allow you to follow up on any future opportunities in the event the current one does not work out.

10

EVALUATING A JOB OFFER

Evaluating a job offer involves considering several factors to ensure that the role aligns with your professional and personal goals. Items to consider when evaluating a job offer include:

Compensation and Benefits

- Does the salary meet your financial needs and reflect your experience and market value?

- Are there opportunities for bonuses and salary increases?

- What do health insurance options look like? Are they comprehensive and affordable?

- Does the company offer retirement plans like 401(k) or pensions, and do they provide matching contributions?

- Consider other perks like stock options, tuition reimbursement, wellness programs, and employee discounts.

Work-Life Balance

- Are the expected work hours reasonable? Is there flexibility in scheduling?

- What amount of paid time does the company offer, and what are its policies on sick leave, parental leave, and other types of leave?

- Does the company offer remote work options or flexible work arrangements?

Job Role and Responsibilities

- Does the role align with your skills, experience, and career goals?

- Are there clear paths for career advancement within the company?

- Does the company provide opportunities for professional development and further education?

Company Culture and Values

- Is the company culture collaborative, inclusive, and supportive?

- Do the company's values and mission resonate with your own?

- How well do you think you'll fit in with your potential colleagues and supervisors?

Job Security and Stability

- Is the company financially stable and growing?

- Is the company a leader in its industry, or is it facing significant challenges?

Location and Commute

- Is the commute manageable for you, or are there remote work options available?

- If the job requires relocation, are relocation benefits offered, and is the new location suitable for your lifestyle?

Finally, evaluate how you feel about the offer on a personal level. Does it excite you or give you any reservations? Can you see yourself thriving in this role and with this company for the foreseeable future?

Evaluating these factors can empower you to make an informed decision about whether to accept a job offer. Remember, it's not just about the salary, but the complete package. By taking the time to ensure it aligns with your professional and personal aspirations.

SALARY NEGOTIATIONS

Salary negotiation is discussing and agreeing on the terms of your compensation with an employer. It typically occurs after receiving a job offer but can also happen during performance reviews for raises or promotions. Asking about a salary too early might make it seem like you're only focused on money rather than the role itself, so avoid bringing up a salary too soon. Wait to discuss salary until the employer raises the topic, and the timing feels right. But it is best to prepare responses to common salary-related questions such as "What are your salary expectations?" and "What was your previous salary?" in advance to avoid hesitation or sounding un-certain. However, in some locations, laws prohibit employers from asking about your current or past salary; therefore, research your local laws to understand your rights. If the laws or company culture don't require disclosure of past salaries, it's best to focus on future expectations. If appropriate, be prepared to share your salary expectations if the interviewer mentions salary first. However, deflect salary discussions if the interviewer asks too early.

Example: "I'm happy to discuss salary, but I'd love to learn more about the role and responsibilities first to ensure alignment."

Your employer will expect salary discussions once they offer you the job. This is the best time to ask detailed questions about compensation, benefits, and perks.

Approaching salary negotiations can feel challenging, but with preparation and confidence, you can navigate them as negotiating your salary shows confidence and an understanding of your value. It is helpful to keep in mind that most employers expect candidates to negotiate, so failing to do so might leave money on the table.

Do your research and understand market rates. Use resources like Glassdoor and LinkedIn Salary to find salary ranges for similar roles in your industry, location, and experience level. Research the company's compensation practices and financial health to set realistic expectations. Also consider your experience level, education, certifications, and unique skills when evaluating your market value.

When negotiating your salary, it is important to look beyond the base salary and assess the full compensation package, including benefits like health insurance, retirement contributions, bonuses, paid time off, and perks such as remote work flexibility or professional development funds. Understanding and negotiating the full compensation package ensures you secure a deal that aligns with your worth and needs, such as remote work options and professional development.

It is best to negotiate after you have received a formal offer or when asked about salary expectations. If possible, allow the employer to mention a number first. Express gratitude for the offer and discuss your expectations. Avoid mentioning any personal financial obligations as a justification for your expectations. Be ready to showcase how your skills, experience, and accomplishments make you an asset to the company and emphasize the value you bring to the organization rather than focusing on salary.

Example: "I'm confident my skills in [specific area] and my track record of [specific achievements] will make a significant impact on your team."

Always provide a salary range rather than a single number to allow flexibility and show openness to negotiation by stating you're willing to consider the full compensation package (bonuses, additional vacation days, or professional growth opportunities), or propose revisiting your salary after a probationary period or specific performance milestones. Provide honest answers to questions without undervaluing yourself.

Pay attention to the employer's reasoning if they can't meet your request. Avoid being confrontational and approach negotiations as a collaborative conversation. If the salary is non-negotiable, focus on other areas like additional vacation days, professional development funds, and flexible working arrangements, or propose revisiting your salary after a probationary period or specific performance milestones.

Whatever the offer, even if it is attractive, take the time to review it. If the offer meets your minimum expectations, accept it. Consider asking for time to think or propose a counteroffer. However, remember to keep the discussion professional and value driven. If the offer doesn't align with your worth or goals, respectfully decline it.

Ensure you clearly document the final salary, benefits, and any negotiated terms in the offer letter before committing. Salary negotiations are important, as they can help ensure you're compensated fairly for your skills and contributions. A successful negotiation highlights your confidence and self-awareness of employers, but keep in mind that even small increases in salary can compound over time, significantly impacting your financial trajectory.

By approaching salary negotiations with preparation, confidence, and a focus on mutual benefit, you can secure a compensation package that supports your career and personal goals, while leaving a positive impression on your employer.

11

THE LONG HAUL

Job hunting is difficult for many people. The hunt can feel long and challenging, especially during certain times of the year or for specific industries. When finding the right role doesn't happen immediately, facing rejection can impact confidence and morale, while not knowing when or where you'll land a role can create anxiety, especially without a professional support network. Plus, the constant effort of applying, networking, and interviewing can lead to burnout. But it's important to remember that you are not alone in feeling like this.

To help stay motivated, set realistic targets, such as applying to a certain number of jobs, reaching out to a specific number of contacts, or attending networking events each week. Dedicate consistent blocks of time each day to job search activities, including applications, research, and follow-ups and use tools like job application trackers or spreadsheets to monitor progress and deadlines. Use SMART goals (Specific, Measurable, Achievable, Relevant, Time-bound) to stay focused and track progress. Every application you submit, every connection you make, and every interview you attend is a step closer to your goal. In addition, each rejection is a step closer to finding the right fit.

Even if you feel confident about a specific role, continue applying for other positions to keep your options open. Explore different roles and industries that align with your skills to maximize opportunities.

Use any interview feedback to improve your applications and performance. If you're not hearing from applications or interviews, seek feedback from recruiters, mentors, or colleagues to improve your approach. Use constructive criticism to refine your resume, cover letter, or interview skills. If you're not seeing results, evaluate what might need improvement, reconsider your resume, cover letter, networking tactics, or the roles you're applying for.

Besides your job search, work on building up your professional skills. Use platforms like Coursera, LinkedIn Learning, or Udemy to enhance skills relevant to your target roles. Industry-specific certifications can make your application more competitive (e.g., PMP for project management, Google Analytics for marketing).

Weigh the pros and cons of each job offer carefully, considering how it fits into your long-term career goals. Be open to roles that might not be a perfect match but offer growth opportunities or industry connections. Picture yourself in your ideal role, thriving and contributing, using this visualization to remind yourself of why you're putting in the effort and how the outcome will be worth it.

By staying motivated and maintaining a balanced, focused approach, you can turn even a prolonged job search into a rewarding journey of personal and professional growth. Success may not happen overnight, but your perseverance will lead to the right opportunity.

Remember, even small actions build momentum. The right opportunity might take time to find, but staying motivated during a long job hunt is essential for maintaining focus, overcoming setbacks, and ultimately achieving your goals. Acknowledge achievements like getting an interview, receiving positive feedback, or learning a new skill. Instead of worrying about outcomes, concentrate on improving your resume, enhancing your interview skills, and networking.

Each rejection is not a reflection of your worth, but it's a redirection toward something better suited to your skills and aspirations. Believe in your abilities, stay committed to your growth, and trust that your hard work will pay off. The process may be tough, but so are you, and the career you're working toward is worth the effort. Keep believing in yourself, and incredible opportunities will come your way.

THANK YOU

Dear Reader,

Thank you so much for taking the time to read my book. Your support means the world to me. If you found value in this book, I'd be incredibly grateful if you could take a few minutes to leave a review on Amazon or Goodreads. Your feedback not only helps me improve, but also helps other readers discover the book. Whether it's a few words or a detailed review, your voice matters and makes a big difference!

Warm regards, R.D. Bennett

12

RESOURCES

ELEVATOR PITCH

Herrity, J. (2024, August 13). *How to give an elevator pitch (With Examples)*. Indeed Career Guide. https://www.indeed.com/career-advice/interviewing/how-to-give-an-elevator-pitch-examples

Stojanovic, M. (2024, December 10). *9 Elevator pitch examples to ensure you stand out*. Big Interview. https://resources.biginterview.com/interviews-101/elevator-pitch-examples/

Ramki, H. (2024, November 26). *11 actually great elevator pitch examples and how to make yours*. https://zapier.com/blog/elevator-pitch-example/?msockid=1206e760c-d3366970868e838cc846793

HANDBILL

(5) The handbill as a networking tool | LinkedIn. (2019, September 20). https://www.linkedin.com/pulse/handbill-networking-tool-nancy-mellem/

Nachsin, W. (2024, December 11). *What's a handbill, and who needs one? | Life Working®*. Life Working®. https://www.lifeworking.com/blog/whats-a-handbill-and-who-needs-one

RESUMES

Buckner, L. (2024, December 5). *What to include on a Resume: key elements, tips and examples.* Indeed, Career Guide. https://www.indeed.com/career-advice/resumes-cover-letters/what-to-include-on-a-resume

Eilers, C. (2024, September 16). What to put on a Resume (20+ best things to include). *ResumeLab.* https://resumelab.com/resume/what-to-include

Leitch, C. (2022, May 31). *How to structure your résumé (Sections and Examples).* https://www.careeraddict.com/include-structure-cv

INTERVIEW QUESTIONS

Clark, B. (2024, January 27). *Top 40 essential interview questions and answers.* Career Sidekick. https://careersidekick.com/what-to-say-in-a-job-interview-questions-and-answers/

Indeed Editorial Team. (2024, September 9). *Top 20 interview questions (With sample answers)*. Indeed Career Guide. https://www.indeed.com/career-advice/interviewing/top-20-interview-questions

Oliver, V. (2024, October 29). *10 Common job interview questions and how to answer them*. Harvard Business Review. https://hbr.org/2021/11/10-common-job-interview-questions-and-how-to-answer-them

Team, G. (2020, June 24). *50 most common interview questions | Glassdoor blog*. Glassdoor US. https://www.glassdoor.com/blog/common-interview-questions/

Birt, J. (2024, September 9). *48 questions to ask about the company during an interview*. Indeed Career Guide. https://www.indeed.com/career-advice/interviewing/questions-to-ask-a-company

77 Questions to ask the interviewer during an interview – Glassdoor US. (2024, June 25). Glassdoor US. https://www.glassdoor.com/blog/guide/questions-to-ask/

Third Party Resources

AREA	COMPANY	AREA	COMPANY
Interview Preparation	Pramp Interview stream	Keyword Search	Google trends
Keyword search	Google sheet Excel Huntr JibberJobber	Resumes	Canva Resume genius Jobscan
Salary Evaluation	Glassdoor LinkedIn salary	Training	Coursera LinkedIn Learning Udemy Verizon edx
Writing assistance	Grammarly Google docs ProWritingAid		

US Online Job Platforms

PLATFORM	WEBSITE
General	
LinkedIn	www.linkedin.com
Glassdoor	www.glassdoor
Indeed	www.indeed.com
Ziprecruiter	www.ziprecruiter.com
Monster	www.monster.com

PLATFORM	WEBSITE
Tech	
Dice	www.dice.com
Upwork	www.upwork.com
Stack overflow	www.stackoverflow.com
Creative	
Behance	www.behance.net
Dribble	www.dribble.com
Mediabistro	www.mediabistro.com
Nonprofit	
Idealist	www.idealist.org
Devex	www.devex.com
Non-Profit Jobs	www.nonprofitjobs.org
National Council of Nonprofits	www.careers.councilofnonprofits.org
Work for Good	www.workforgood.org
Remote	
We Work Remotely	www.weworkremotely.com
Remote.co	www.remotejobs.io
FlexJobs	www.flexjobs.com
Working Nomads	www.workingnomads.com
US government jobs	
USAJobs	www.usajobs.gov

OTHER BOOKS BY R. D. BENNETT

Find other books by R. D. Bennett on any of the following websites:

www.rd-bennett.com

www.snowhillamerica.com

ABOUT THE AUTHOR

R. D. Bennett is a nonfiction writer based in Virginia, where she lives with her husband, daughter, and two lovable dogs. With a passion for learning and a deep interest in topics that inspire and support others, she brings a fresh perspective. Embracing a newfound joy for writing, she is excited to connect with readers and grow with each project.

www.ingramcontent.com/pod-product-compliance
Lightning Source LLC
Chambersburg PA
CBHW071514120626
46550CB00006B/2227